America Is Born

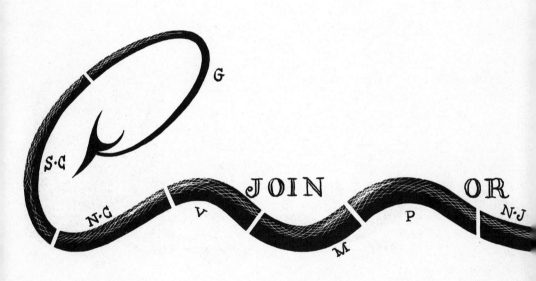

ILLUSTRATED BY
LEONARD EVERETT FISHER

AMERICA
IS BORN

A HISTORY FOR PETER

BY
GERALD W. JOHNSON

WILLIAM MORROW AND COMPANY

LIBRARY EDITION 1968

RESPONSIVE ENVIRONMENTS CORP.
ENGLEWOOD CLIFFS, N.J. 07632

Contents

A Letter to

Peter van den Honert

for whom this book was written.

Dear Peter:

You were born in the State of Massachusetts and that makes you a citizen both of the United States and the State of Massachusetts. The law says so, and since the law was written many years before you were born, you had nothing to do with it. Just being born here made you a citizen of the United States and nobody can deny it.

But the law did not make you an American. Many people think it did, but they are wrong; that part of the law does not even mention the word *American*. Citizens of the United States are, in fact, called Americans, but many other people live in America too. Canadians and Mexicans, for example, have as much right to be called Americans as you and I. The

United States grew so fast and became so strong that people in Europe fell into the habit of forgetting the people in the other countries of America when they spoke of Americans.

So you see being an American is not exactly the same as being a citizen—it is that, but it is something more. The law can make you a citizen, and people will call you an American because you are a citizen of the United States. Citizens of the United States have done things that other people have remembered. It isn't the law that makes you an American; it is the fact that you are connected with the things done in America that nobody forgets.

This book tells of some of those things and tries to explain how they all fit together to make a story that has a beginning and a middle, but no end as yet, because it is still going on. You yourself, Peter, are part of that story, and by the time you have a grandson, you will have added something to it that you can tell him but that I cannot tell you, because it hasn't happened yet.

That is what being an American means: being part of a continued story that goes back from you to George Washington, and beyond him to Captain John Smith, and beyond John Smith to Christopher Columbus. Part of the story is very fine, and other parts are very bad; but they all belong to it, and if

Peter van den Honert

you leave out the bad parts you will never understand it all. Yet you must understand it if you are to make your part one of the fine parts, which is what every father and mother and grandparent hope and expect of a boy.

G. W. J.

Baltimore, 1958

America Is Born

CHAPTER ONE

The Unknown Land

FIVE HUNDRED years ago the land that is now the United States had not a single city, nor even a brick house; not a paved road, not a factory, not a ploughed field. Of course there were no railroads or automobiles or airplanes, for those things had not been invented; but in other parts of the world there were plenty of cities and roads and fields. There were canals with barges on them, and rivers with great ships. There were workshops where skillful men made beautiful and useful things. There were books and pictures, fine clothes, fine horses and carriages — most of the things that people needed to live in comfort.

But that was in the Eastern Hemisphere. If you take a globe of the world and draw a line from the North Pole down the middle of the Atlantic Ocean to the South Pole and then up through the middle of the Pacific back to the North Pole, that part of the globe that contains Europe, Asia, and Africa is the Eastern Hemisphere, and there lived the people who had discovered or invented most of the things that we use every day.

In our half of the world, which we call the Western Hemisphere, there was no civilization five hundred years ago except in Mexico and Peru, where people built cities with houses of stone and knew how to carve statues and paint pictures. They had a kind of writing, very different from ours, but still writing; they knew arithmetic and geometry, and they had engineers who built large and wonderful temples and palaces for their kings.

But in what is now the United States there were no people except those we call Indians. They were savages with dark skins — not black, but copper-colored — and there were not many of them for so large a stretch of land.

Here and there the Indians had cleared away the forest from some small spots, but in general the land was covered with great trees. They came down almost to the water's edge on the Atlantic coast, and they stretched back over a flat plain, in some places narrow but in others extending for hundreds of miles, until the hills began. Trees covered the hills too, for many miles, until the hills rose into mountains. These mountains were not one single range, but many ranges, most of them running side by side, but some crisscrossing. We call the whole system by an Indian name, the Appalachians, and the different ranges by other names, such as the Blue Ridge, the Alleghenies, the Great Smokies, and others. The Appalachians are fairly high mountains, rising to more than 6000 feet in what is now New Hampshire and to nearly 7000 in North Carolina; but they are not so high that trees cannot grow, even on their tops.

The forest kept on across the mountains and down into the valley on the western side. There the land sloped gradually for hundreds of miles to a great river in the middle of the continent, a river so huge that the Indians called it the Mississippi, which in their language meant "Father of Waters." On the western side of the Mississippi the land sloped up again, but the slope was so gradual that you would hardly notice it and might think that the country was quite flat. Still, it was slowly rising, and some hundreds of miles west of the Mississippi it broke into another mountain system, and this time a huge one.

People, especially in the East, have the habit of calling them the Rocky Mountains, but the fact is that the Rockies are only a small part of the whole system. The mountains go on, range after range, almost to the Pacific Ocean, and in places they are so high that no trees can grow on their highest peaks, which in California rise to nearly 15,000 feet. That is almost three miles up, and it is so cold and windy up there that nothing can grow; the peaks are bare rock, the rock is almost straight up and down, but where it is fairly level the snow lies and doesn't melt all summer.

At the far western edge of the continent the last mountain range slopes down steeply to hills that are lower and lower until one comes to the coast of the Pacific Ocean. This is the shape of the United States as one goes from east to west — up from the Atlantic to the Appalachians, down to the Mississippi River, up again to the Rockies, and down again to the Pacific. It is very large — almost 3000 miles from east to west and almost 1600 miles from north to south — and parts of it are so different from one another that they do not seem to be the same country. For example, some hundreds of miles west of the Mississippi River the forest stopped, because the soil and the rainfall were not right for growing trees; but grass grew there and in places was so high that a man on horseback could barely see above it. If you looked at him from a little distance you could not see his horse at all. As the land grew higher, the grass grew shorter until, on what we call the High Plains, close to the Rocky Mountains and about 4000 feet high, all that was left was buffalo grass, growing close to the ground. It got its name because it was fine food for the wild animals that the first settlers called buffalo (actually they were bison), and later for cattle. Then in certain places, especially in the Southwest, there was so little water that even the buffalo grass could not grow and the land was sandy or stony desert, with nothing growing except a few desert plants, such as cactus, mesquite, and sagebrush.

Five hundred years ago all this was unknown to anyone in the Eastern Hemisphere. In Europe men didn't even know that America existed. They knew, or at least educated people knew, that the world was round, but they supposed that water extended from the coast of Spain to the coast of China with no land except, perhaps, some islands in between. They all thought that the water was so wide that nobody could get across it.

This was not as silly as it seems to us today. There were no steamships and no very large sailing ships. Many of the ships they had were moved by oars, not by sails. To go far out to sea in such craft was dangerous, and only a few ships were large enough to carry water and food for a long voyage.

Then there was the difficulty of finding one's way. When you are out of sight of land the sea looks the same in all directions. Of course, the sun rises in the east and sets in the west, so if you could see which way the sun was moving you knew which way your ship was going. At night you could steer by the North Star, which in the old days was called Polaris because it was almost over the North Pole. As long as your ship was pointed toward the North Star you knew that to your right was east, to your left west, and at your back was south.

But suppose the sky was cloudy and the air foggy, as it often is at sea for many days together. You could see neither sun nor stars, and what then? Sailors had solved that problem by what they called the compass. They had discovered that certain chunks of iron ore, which they called lodestones, were natural magnets, and if you took a steel needle and rubbed it on a lodestone, the needle, if free to move, would turn until it pointed almost north and south. To make it free to move they fastened the needle to something light, such as a bit of cork, and let it float in a bowl of water. They used a round bowl, which they fastened firmly on the ship at a place where the man steering could see it, and on its rim they cut notches, or made marks, dividing it into 360 equal parts, to represent the 360 degrees of a circle. One

18

notch was in line with the prow of the ship, and counting from that, Notch Number 90 pointed to the right and Number 180 pointed toward the stern. As the ship turned, the rim of the bowl turned with it, but the floating needle did not. So the steersman knew that if the needle pointed to Notch Zero the ship was going north, while if it pointed to Notch 90 the direction was west, and if it pointed to 180 it was south.

On a modern compass north is marked, not by a zero, but by a fleur-de-lis. The reason is that the Italians, who developed the mariner's compass, found that in Italy the needle always pointed toward the Alps, north of Italy. They guessed that it was pointing at something beyond the mountains, the Italian word for which was *tramontane.* So they marked that point with a T, instead of a zero. Later compass makers began to make the T fancier and fancier, until finally they turned it into the fleur-de-lis, which looks something like a very fancy T.

Yet even with the compass, sailing out of sight of land was pretty risky business, for while you could always tell which way you were going you had no good way of telling how far you had gone. You could make a rough guess by judging the speed of the ship through the water and multiplying it by the number of hours you had been sailing, but that was only a very rough guess, and men didn't like to risk their lives on it.

So, for the most part, the ships in those days kept pretty close to shore, where the pilot could see some kind of landmark, a high hill, perhaps, or when close to shore a church steeple or a very tall tree, which would tell him where he was. Even so, some daring sailors had gone a long way out. They had discovered Iceland in the north, and the Canary and Cape Verde islands in the south. Some had even pushed down the whole length of Africa, to the Cape of Good Hope.

But of America they knew nothing at all and for a long time nobody really cared to know. They had enough to do in building up Europe, where the great nations of France, Spain, and Austria were beginning to take shape. As yet the little island of Britain didn't amount to much: it was off to one side, and nobody paid much attention to what was going on there. Holland was thought to be more important, and so were the half dozen kingdoms into which Italy was split up. Few Europeans guessed that in that island of Britain a set of ideas was slowly developing that later would make England great. Through England, these ideas would spread to cover a continent containing one country as large as all Europe except for Russia, and with more inhabitants than any European country except Russia.

Most of the men of Europe thought that what lay beyond the rim of the world, as men viewed it from the coasts of Portugal and Ireland, was nobody's business. Vast America lay unknown and unsuspected. The great forest trees sprang up, lived for centuries, died, and were followed by others. Wild animals roamed through the woods, hardly disturbed by the bows and arrows of a few copper-colored men. Storms howled across the land, such storms as Europe hardly knew. Fiercer heats than Europe knew baked it in the summers, and fiercer cold than any part of Europe knew, except the extreme north, locked it in ice during the winters. The vast Mississippi rolled down to the sea bearing no kind of boat except an occasional Indian canoe. The island of Manhattan was dense forest, swamps spread where Chicago and New Orleans stand now, no civilized man had ever looked upon San Francisco Bay.

Vast, dark, unknown, the land lay for thousands of years, hardly used at all by men and women, for the few Indians never knew how to use it and never cared to learn. The wolf, the bear, the panther, and the bison flourished and increased faster than people. The land waited for a master who did not come for a long, long time.

❀   ❀   ❀

In the year 1453 something happened thousands of miles to the east that led to the discovery of America. For many hundreds of years there had been fairly constant warfare between the Christians of Europe and the Moslems (the followers of Mohammed), who came out of Asia, first in the armies of the Arabs and later in those of the Turks. The great fortress protecting Europe, and at the same time the great gateway between Europe and Asia, was the city sometimes called Byzantium, sometimes Constantinople, and today Istanbul.

For more than eleven centuries Asiatics had been trying to capture it, without success; and for eleven centuries Europeans had poured through it now and then to carry war into Asia. But between fights it was the great market town where cloth from Flanders, sword blades from Spain, wines and leather from France and Italy, were exchanged for ivories and silks and muslins and spices from Asia. In war or in peace, Byzantium was important, immensely important, to all the rest of Europe. The Scythians knew it, the Persians knew it, the Mongols knew it, and all of them tried to take it. The Moslems knew it best of all, and they fought for nearly seven hundred years to get it. Finally, in 1453, they succeeded, and the first thing they did was to shut off Europe from Asia. Some trade was permitted, but only on terms fixed by the Turks, and those terms were not easy. They were so harsh, in fact, that all over Europe people began to long for some other way of getting to the East.

Where this state of affairs hit the Europeans hardest was in their eating. After all, silks and muslins and ivory chessmen and pearls and jewels were fine things, but one could get along without them. What the people in Europe wanted most of all from the East was spice. Salt they had, but nothing else to season their food — no pepper, nor cloves, nor cinnamon, nor nutmeg, all of which came from the East. What we now know as the Moluccas were then called the Spice Islands. They lay far beyond the country of the Turks, but their spices were brought into Europe through Byzantium and the Turks could, and did, cut them off unless the Europeans paid very high prices for them.

One reason why people were so fond of spices was the fact that their meat was usually pretty bad. In those days they knew very little about keeping food. Of course they had no electric refrigerators and they had not yet learned how to make ice in summer. They had no iron cookstoves and the cooking was done at open fireplaces. It was usually bad, even in kings' palaces and the houses of rich noblemen. So they used great quantities of spices to give the food a better taste, and they hated having to beg the Turks to let the spices come through.

Some people had always believed that there was a way to the Spice Islands by sea, without going anywhere near Turkey. In fact, a Greek named Herodotus wrote a book in which he quoted an assertion made by some Egyptian sailors that Africa had an end and that they had reached it. Herodotus himself doubted that statement because these men said they came to a place where, as they sailed west, they had the sun on the right hand, and Herodotus couldn't believe that there was any such place. Of course, if you are below the equator when you go west the sun *is* on your right; but he didn't know about the equator.

However, after 1453, when Byzantium fell to the Turks, people began to take more interest in these old tales. They now had a real reason for wishing to get to the East by sea, so anyone with an idea of how to do it was listened to as he had never been before. Somewhat before the success of the Turks there was a prince in Portugal, a brother of the king, who became so much interested in geography that he spent most of his life studying it. He studied the compass and made improvements in it. He studied shipbuilding and designed ships that were stronger and more seaworthy than any others. He spent a great deal of money sending ships down the coast of Africa. His captains discovered the Madeira Islands and the Cape Verde Islands, and they almost reached the equator. All the new lands they discovered they claimed for Portugal, and some of them proved to be very rich, so all the other kings of Europe began to look at Portugal enviously and to wish that they had somebody like this Prince Henry the Navigator to help them find new kingdoms.

When Prince Henry died, an Italian boy of fourteen was somewhere at sea learning the trade of a sailor. He learned it so well that by the time he was thirty years old he was a famous captain. He liked Portugal and at thirty-one he decided to make his home in the city of Lisbon, where he married a Portuguese girl. This Italian sailor came to be known in Portugal, not by his Italian name of Cristoforo Colombo, but by its Spanish form, Cristobal Colon. Of course in English it is Christopher Columbus.

As a sailor he heard much talk about this idea of going to the Spice Islands by sea. Some claimed that the way to do it was to go north, sailing around Norway; others said no, the thing to do was to go south, sailing around the southern end of Africa. It was known that beyond the tip of Norway the cold was terrible, and the sea was full of ice. On the other hand, it was known that as one sailed down the coast of Africa the climate got hotter and hotter, and

some believed that you would finally come to a place
where the sea would be boiling. It was still some
years before a Portugese sailor named Diaz would
sail right through the tropic zone, coming to cooler
weather and at last to the Cape of Good Hope and
the end of Africa.

Columbus, though, had an idea of his own. If the
world was round, as the wisest men of the time
agreed, why go either north or south? Why not sail
due west? If the world was round and if you sailed
long enough, you would be bound to bump into the
coast of Asia somewhere. He asked the king (not
the brother of Prince Henry, for he had died years
before, but another king, who was much less interested in such matters) to fit out a ship and let him
try to reach the East that way. It was known that
beyond India lay a great many islands, known in
Europe as the Indies, and it was these that Columbus proposed to reach.

The king listened at first, but then all sorts of
people rose up with all sorts of objections. Some said
that it had never been proved that the world was
round. Nobody really knew what lay beyond the
horizon, and if it turned out that the world was flat,
a ship sailing west might sail off the edge. Others
said that even if the idea was good, it would cost too
much. Many said that Columbus was crazy and the

king should not encourage a madman, certainly not give him a great deal of money to try out such a wild scheme.

So the king of Portugal made the worst mistake of his life, by listening to people who thought they knew more than a man who had been studying the subject for many years. He refused to help Columbus and thereby missed great riches, a great extension of his kingdom, and great fame in the world. Yet of all the kings in Europe he should have been the one best able to understand what Columbus was talking about, because Prince Henry the Navigator had already shown Portugal what wonderful things might be done by boldly striking out and exploring the unknown parts of the world. Because of this mistake he is remembered as someone who showed that even a king may be a silly fellow.

When he found that the king of Portugal would do nothing, Columbus tried others and at last went across the mountains into Spain. Shortly before that time Spain, which had been divided into two kingdoms, had become one country when Ferdinand, King of Aragon, married Isabella, Queen of Castile. After their marriage they ruled as Ferdinand and Isabella, King and Queen of Spain.

If the truth must be told, these were not very nice people. Ferdinand, especially, was a bloody tyrant.

He drove the Moors and the Jews out of Spain, and he set up the Inquisition to persecute everybody who disagreed with his religion. Isabella was not much better; she consented to her husband's cruel treatment of the Moors and Jews and even added some ideas of her own.

But it cannot be denied that they were smart. They had taken note of how the Portuguese were drawing riches from their possessions in Africa, and they wished the Spanish could do likewise. So they were inclined to listen when Columbus came to them with his idea of sailing west. They did not accept his plan at once, though. Here, as in Portugal, there were many people, wise in their own conceit, who cried out against Columbus's scheme as crazy, useless, and probably sinful. Some, no doubt, really did believe that he was a wild man, but a great many were thinking of themselves, not of Columbus. In those days nearly everybody was trying to get something out of the king and queen, and they thought that if money were given to Columbus there would be that much less for them. So they did everything they could to oppose him.

They were successful for a long time. Columbus hung about the court for four years. He did not have money enough of his own to fit out an expedition; in fact, he spent about all he had while waiting for the king and queen to make up their minds. He had almost given up hope and had decided to leave and try somewhere else, when the decision came. There is a tradition that it was the queen who saved Columbus. The court treasurer had said, falsely, that there was not money enough in the royal treasury to fit out the ships; but Queen Isabella had become really interested and believed in Columbus. The story is — but nobody knows that it is true — that she said if there was no money in the treasury, she would borrow it, giving her jewels as security.

At any rate, early in the year 1492 Spain decided to try it. Columbus was given the money. He lost no time. He was given the money in April, and by August he had not one but three ships fitted out. On August 3 he sailed from the little port of Palos, Spain.

Yet to say that Columbus had three ships is enough to make a modern sailor laugh; he wouldn't call those things ships. The United States Navy looks on a destroyer as a small ship, and it *is* small when you put it beside a cruiser, a battleship, or an aircraft carrier. Yet you could have loaded all three of Columbus's ships on one destroyer and had lots of room to spare.

Two of them, named the *Nina* and the *Pinta*, were what the Portuguese called caravels; the third, named

29

the *Santa Maria* was a *nao,* or ship. The *Santa Maria* was a little larger than the others, but not much. Columbus did not write down much about his ships, so we do not know their exact measurements, but it seems likely that none was over 75 feet long, and the largest, the *Santa Maria,* is supposed to have rated about 100 tons. To gain some idea of what this means, compare the figures with those of the *Queen Elizabeth,* the largest ship in the world as this book is written — *Santa Maria,* 75 feet and 100 tons; *Queen Elizabeth,* 987 feet and 83,000 tons.

These were not by any means the best ships of the time. There were many larger and stronger, but the king and queen were not disposed to risk a fine ship on an adventure so dangerous, and they put Columbus off with just as little as they could manage. Yet as it turned out this was not altogether a bad thing. After he made his first voyage, Columbus himself said that big ships were not the best for exploring; smaller ones could sail closer to the coast, and slip through places where the big ones could not go without striking the bottom; so you could learn more in a small ship.

At the same time, the idea of crossing the Atlantic in vessels as small as those of Columbus was enough to frighten brave men. In 1492 there were thousands of sailors willing to risk crossing those bodies of water nearly surrounded by land: the Mediterranean Sea, the Black Sea, the Red Sea, the North Sea, and so on. But when it came to trying to cross the limitless body of water stretching west from Europe, which they called the Ocean Sea, there had been none before Columbus who had done it and lived to tell the tale. It is probable that in Palos, on August 3, 1492, there were few who expected ever to see Columbus or any of his men again.

Indeed, the men themselves began to doubt that they would ever see their homes again, as the voyage went on and on. All through the month of August they sailed westward, and all through the month of September. They got into the trade winds that blow steadily from east to west, and the sailors began to wonder how they could hope to get back against these winds. By the end of September their fright was almost panic, and Columbus, when he made his calculations at noon every day, began to cut down the number of miles he figured that they had actually sailed, so that the men would not realize how far they were from Spain. At last it came to the point when some of the men were in favor of committing mutiny: that is, rising against the Captain and forcing him to turn back. If he would not, some were in favor of throwing him overboard and turning back anyhow.

October came, and they were still sailing west, but Columbus was having more and more trouble with the crews. He threatened, and when threats began to fail he begged and pleaded with them to go just a little farther. Finally, on October 11, the two Pinzon brothers, captains of the *Nina* and the *Pinta*, came to him and said they could do no more. They were brave men, but they were losing control of their crews, for, as they said, "We have run 800 leagues and have found no land, and these people say that they are going to be lost." To them Columbus replied, "Do me this favor! Stay with me this day and night, and if I don't bring you to land before

day, cut off my head and you shall return." But on October 12 they sighted land.

Many years later an American poet, Joaquin Miller, wrote some verses about this incident which are famous. The poem begins:

> Behind him lay the gray Azores,
>   Behind the Gates of Hercules;
> Before him not the ghost of shores,
>   Before him only shoreless seas.
> The good mate said: "Now must we pray,
>   For lo! the very stars are gone.
> Brave Admiral, speak, what shall I say?"
> "Why, say 'Sail on! sail on! and on!' "

Americans like this poem because it is a fine expression of the courage that made the discovery of America possible.

Columbus, of course, thought he had arrived at some unknown part of Asia or at one of the islands off the Asian coast. The country was new and his instruments were not very good. From the records he left, we are not quite sure which of the many islands in the West Indies was the one he first saw, but we think it was what is now called Watling Island, one of the Bahamas. At any rate, Columbus went on and discovered Haiti, which he named Hispaniola, and Cuba. There is no doubt about this, because he described them both well enough for us to recognize them.

He was amazed and delighted with what he saw, but he couldn't find any places like those that had been described by the Europeans who had traveled in the East. This is no wonder, since he was still on the other side of the world from India, although he didn't know it. He was so sure he knew where he was that he named the whole group of islands the Indies, and he called the people he found there Indians. It was years before the truth came out, and by that time people were used to the names and they have stuck ever since. The only change they made was to call them the West Indies, while those islands that really were near Asia became the East Indies; but the people kept the name of Indians and are so called to this day.

If Columbus and his men were amazed, the Indians were even more amazed. At first they did not believe that the Spaniards were men at all, but thought them some kind of gods; and as neither the sailors nor the natives could speak the other's language they had a hard time making each other understand, and got all sorts of wrong ideas. For one thing, Columbus never discovered his mistake, and for the rest of his life he believed that he had reached

Asia. But he collected all sorts of strange plants and animals and birds and persuaded some Indians to go back with him to prove that he had discovered, as it came to be called, a New World. He found some gold, too, and a few pearls; and as he and his men learned the Indian language they were told all sorts of stories about wonderful lands farther to the west. A good many of these tales were lies, but after what they had seen Columbus and his men were ready to believe anything.

So they sailed back to Spain, getting there early in 1493, and you can imagine the excitement — no, you can't imagine it, for nothing like Columbus's voyage has happened in our time. The first thing that occurred to Ferdinand and Isabella was that they must keep this news secret, for fear that the Portuguese and the French and the English and other nations that had ships would rush in and seize the new country, which they wished to keep for Spain. So they kept Columbus's report locked up and allowed nothing to be printed. Then they made haste to fit out another and larger expedition for Columbus and they sent other sailors to examine the new country.

But of course you couldn't keep a thing like that secret very long. Although nobody saw Columbus's report, the sailors talked, and their families and friends talked, and travelers in Spain heard the talk and took the story back to other countries. So within a few years word spread all over Europe that there was a New World across the Atlantic and bold sailors of many nations set out to find it. Among them was an Italian named Amerigo Vespucci, who made four voyages in the next few years, and then wrote a book about his travels which was printed at the little town of St. Dié, in France, and was the first real story of the discoveries that people outside of Spain had ever seen. It was in Latin and the author's name was given in the Latin form, Americus Vespucius. Most people thought that Vespucius had discovered the land himself, so they gave it the name of "Americus' land," which soon became America.

By the time the truth was known, the name America was so well established that it couldn't be changed to Columbia, which would have been the right name. America it has remained ever since.

Poor Columbus, in fact, lost a great deal more than the right to have his name given to the new country. As soon as the king and queen began to favor him, others became jealous and envious; they told Ferdinand and Isabella all kinds of lies. They said Columbus was concealing most of the gold that he found and that he intended to make himself a king. The Spanish monarchs were the kind that would believe stories against anybody; so in the end they had Columbus arrested and sent home in chains. Years later his son proved that the stories were a pack of lies, but by that time Columbus had died, poor and neglected.

But his name has endured, as the name of one of the most famous men in the world.

The Spaniards, getting there first, did very well for themselves in the New World. They spread rapidly through the West Indies and pushed on to Mexico. There they found a very different country and very different people. The Aztecs, who lived in Mexico, were not naked savages by any means; they could read and write; they had great cities built of stone; they had artists and astronomers and mathematicians; they knew how to work metals, to refine gold, to smelt copper, to make weapons. Yet for some strange reason they had never invented a wheel, so their best machines were a long way behind those of Europe.

A man named Cortes, a very hard character, was one of those who came to America a dozen years after Columbus's first voyage. The story goes that Cortes, with 500 men, conquered Mexico, but that is not quite right. It is true that he had only 500 Spaniards, but at the moment when he landed there was a civil war raging among the Aztecs and half of them joined Cortes and helped him. At that, he was a bold and determined fellow; as soon as he had landed his Spaniards he set fire to the ships that had brought them and burned them completely. The idea was to make the Spaniards fight bravely, for if they were tempted to run away they could not, because there was nowhere to run. With no ships they could not get away from Mexico, so they had to conquer or die.

They conquered and gained immense riches. One item given as a present to Cortes by Montezuma, king of the Aztecs, was a circular plate of gold, representing the sun, which the Spaniards described as "large as a carriage wheel" and which they valued at 20,000 *pesos de oro*. A *peso de oro* was a gold coin a little bigger than an American ten-dollar gold piece and worth, in our money, about $11.67. This figure was worked out by the American historian Prescott, whose book, *The Conquest of Mexico,* is not only good history but also one of the finest adventure stories ever written in this country. So the value of this great image of the sun was close to $235,000; and it was only one item in a long list of valuable articles sent at the same time.

When he got other ships, Cortes sent gold to Spain by shiploads. A few years later a man named Pizzaro, very much like Cortes, conquered Peru and sent back even more gold and silver. It made Spain for a time the richest country in Europe.

Yet all the gold and silver, pearls and precious stones, were not worth as much as something the Spaniards hardly noticed in the beginning. The Aztecs were fond of a drink the like of which no one in Europe had ever seen. It was made by boiling a certain substance in water and then whipping it to a froth. The Spaniards tasted it, liked it, and sent some home; and out of that grew a trade more valuable than all the gold mines in both Mexico and Peru. The strange stuff was chocolate.

Cortes was a harsh master. He killed Montezuma and most of his generals, priests, and noblemen, and made slaves of the common people. He divided the land among his officers and soldiers, and with each estate he gave a certain number of Indians to work it, so that the owner could live at ease. To ourselves, who are living in the twentieth century, that seems a pretty dreadful way to act; but all this happened more than four hundred years ago, when most people thought it all right for a king to take anything he was strong enough to take and hold; and Cortes was acting — at least he was supposed to be acting — for the king of Spain.

Ferdinand and Isabella were both dead by the time Mexico was conquered, and their grandson, Charles, was king. He was not the man to worry about what Cortes was doing to the Indians, for he himself at various times fought the French, the Dutch, the Pope, and the Turks. He put the king of France and the Pope in prison and did not hesitate to make slaves of captured Turks. He is less well known as Charles I of Spain than by his other title, Charles V, Holy Roman Emperor. Today that title seems rather a joke, but the man wasn't. Charles V was certainly not holy, and he was not Roman, but there is no doubt that he was an emperor. He conquered most of Europe and terrified all of it.

So in judging Cortes and the other conquistadores (the Spanish word for conquerors) we should keep in mind the old saying, "like master, like man." Humane feelings were not to be expected from officers of Charles V. As a matter of fact, they were not much worse than the others of their time. Later the English and the French were about as hard on the Indians as the Spaniards were. It was a harsh age, and the conquistadores acted pretty much as conquerors of all other nations acted.

Besides, the story is not all blood and tyranny. Rough soldiers conquered the country with great cruelty and had no other thought than to wring wealth out of the wretched inhabitants. But along with them came men of a different sort. One of the finest was Bartolomé de Las Casas, who came to Hispaniola as a planter, but who was so moved by pity for the Indian slaves that after a few years he became a priest and spent the rest of his life fighting the slavery system and trying to secure justice for the Indians. Las Casas was a great and good man, perhaps the greatest and best of the Spaniards who followed Cortes, but there were others who were neither greedy nor cruel. Some were priests, some teachers, some doctors, some scholars. They founded the University of Mexico in 1551, many years before there was an Englishman in North America; they set up schools, they printed books, and they preached Christianity all through Central and South America.

The Spanish conquest had its good as well as its bad side. It horrified the English, who came later, but as much because the English hated the Spaniards as because of the wickedness of the Spanish rule. The English were little, if any, better; but because the history books that most of us read were written by the English, many Americans still believe that the Spaniards were bad beyond all example. It is not true; they were no worse than all the other Europeans, and they had at least two good qualities — they were brave and very strong.

CHAPTER TWO

The People Who Won It

WHEN NEWS of what Columbus had discovered spread around, all the kings in Europe wished to have a share in the New World, but it took most of them a long time to do anything about it. Sending ships across the Atlantic was difficult, dangerous, and very expensive. Few sailors had either knowledge enough or courage enough to make the trip; only the Portuguese, who had gone around Africa all the way to India, were accustomed to long voyages, so at first only the Portuguese seriously tried to rival the Spaniards.

At this time all the kings of Europe were still Roman Catholic, and disputes among them were frequently referred to the Pope. As soon as Columbus made his discovery, Spain applied to the Pope and was given the right to claim all the lands that might be discovered in the Western Hemisphere. This did not suit Portugal at all, and she made such a fuss about it that in 1494 Spain agreed that Portugal, but no other nation, might claim lands beyond a line that the two countries drew on a map. But the only important discovery that Portugal ever made under this agreement was Brazil, which a captain named Cabral discovered by accident in 1500. He was trying to reach the Cape of Good Hope, but when he got off Cape Verde — where the Atlantic Ocean is narrowest — storms drove him so far to the west that he found Brazil. Portugal kept that country for more than three hundred years, and the Brazilians speak Portuguese to this day, although the people in the countries around them all speak Spanish.

But the countries north of Spain — France, Holland, England, Sweden — did not get really interested in America until Cortes began to send back gold by the shipload from Mexico. This was thirty years after Columbus's first voyage, and in the meantime nobody had done much to interfere with the Spaniards and Portuguese. King Henry VII, of England, did hire an Italian sailor named Giovanni Caboto (known to us as John Cabot) to try to find a northerly route to Asia, and he explored the coast from Newfoundland down about as far as the mouth of the Delaware River. A few others made voyages, but none amounted to much. The kings did not get really excited until all that gold began streaming back first from Mexico and a few years later from Peru.

That really waked them up. From about 1550 on, every nation that had ships and sailors began trying to get a foothold in the New World. In the meantime Henry VIII, of England, had quarreled with the Pope and broken away from the Catholic Church. Martin Luther had started the Reformation in Germany and it had spread into Holland. Both the English and the Dutch were seagoing people, so here were two nations who cared nothing about the Pope's orders; the fact that he had given the New World to Spain and Portugal didn't bother them at all. They proposed to take all they could.

France, too, although still a Catholic country, did not propose to be left out. She started somewhat later than the others, but once started she moved faster than either the Dutch or the English. Her representative, Champlain, founded Canada, and in a fairly short time her hunters and woodsmen coming down from the Great Lakes held most of the Mississippi valley, while the English were still strung thinly along the east coast of North America.

But it was when the English came that the part of

history that belongs to the United States really began. Other nations had something to do with the early part, especially Spain, France, Holland, and Sweden; but England drove out France, Holland, and Sweden, and prevented Spain from holding more than the extreme southern and western parts of the country.

So the history of the United States is tied more closely to that of England than of any other country. You cannot know American history well without knowing something of the history of England, for they are parts of the same story.

In 1492 England was not very important in Europe and seemed to be going down rather than up. Four hundred years earlier the island had been conquered by a French duke, William of Normandy, whom we call William the Conqueror. He had the idea that he ought to be king of France. He never made it; but his sons and grandsons and great-grandsons kept trying for many generations, and at one time they actually held a large part of France. By 1492, however, they had been driven out except for the one town of Calais, so the king of England then was ruler over half of one not very large island (the other half was Scotland with its own king), the town of Calais in France, and a strip of land around Dublin, in Ireland, called the Pale.

49

When they were driven off the land in Europe the English took to the sea. By 1492 they were already good sailors and were becoming steadily better. By 1562 the Spaniards themselves were employing one of the English captains, John Hawkins, in the bad trade of transporting Negro slaves from Africa to the West Indies. Later the Spaniards were to wish that this Hawkins had never lived, for he commanded one division of the English fleet that defeated the great Spanish Armada, and he also trained in seamanship a young kinsman named Francis Drake, who lived to become the terror of all Spanish seamen.

But when Cortes was conquering Mexico, and Pizzaro, Peru, neither the Spaniards nor the Portuguese thought much of the English as sailors or fighters. Certainly they did not fear them, and when the two countries divided the western world between them and later persuaded the Pope to ratify the agreement, it did not occur to them to consult either England or Holland. If they feared anybody in Europe it was France, but France at the time did not seem interested.

Yet the very fact that England had been driven out of France forced her to take to the sea. There was nowhere else to go. She had many skilled workmen, especially weavers, and she wanted to exchange her cloth and other things for the products of other countries. So since she couldn't conquer, she began to trade, and trading meant ships. Since the seas around England are much stormier than the Mediterranean, the English ships had to be sturdy, and since they were meant for trading they had to be fast, for the merchant who got there first had the pick of the market.

So the English shipbuilders worked constantly on two things — to make the hull of the ship strong enough to stand the pounding of great waves, and to cut and set the sails in such a way that they would catch the least breath of wind and make the most of it. They did not worry much about size, as long as they got strength and speed, for at that time most of their voyages were short.

The Spanish, on the other hand, making long voyages across the Atlantic and later across the Pacific, were interested in size. Speed did not matter as much as carrying a large cargo, for at that time they had no rivals in the lands to which they sailed. They finally designed a ship that they called the galleon, which was very fine for their purposes — large, roomy, and able to ride out the worst storms in the Atlantic, but slow and not easily turned about.

So in the beginning the Spanish did not worry much about the English ships, even though they were rapidly increasing in numbers. A great Spanish galleon could easily beat any English ship afloat, so why should they worry? Not until many years later did they realize that a galleon attacked by half a dozen English ships at once would be in real trouble; and when they did realize it, it was too late.

But these English, while they were building fast ships and learning to be the best sailors in the world, were doing another thing. They were also building a nation not quite like any other in Europe. Nobody knows exactly how it began, but the English had a different idea about people. Once, like everybody else in Europe, they had the idea that the land and everything on it belonged to the king. The king gave — or it might be better to say, lent — large sections of the land and the people who tilled it to his noblemen: dukes, earls, and barons. In return, the noblemen were bound to bring all their people and fight for the king whenever he commanded them to do so. Each baron, earl, or duke divided his section of land and gave parts of it to knights, who were bound to fight for the baron as the baron was bound to fight for the king. Sometimes a knight gave sections of his lands to squires, or yeomen, who agreed to fight for the knight.

At the bottom of the pile were the people who

worked on the land, plowing, planting, and reaping, tending the sheep and cows and horses, grinding the grain, making the cloth, and waiting on the lord of the manor and his family. These were the serfs, regarded as part of the estate, and bought and sold with the land, much as the trees that grew on it. An estate held from the king or from a baron was called a *foed* (sometimes spelled *feud*), and the whole system was the feudal system.

Everything depended on the serfs, for if they had not worked the land the lords and ladies would have had nothing to eat, no clothes to wear, and no horses to ride. For a very long time the serfs kept working because they did not dare do anything else. In those days there were not many people on the land and few towns or cities. There were a great many wild beasts in the forests and, what was worse, many bands of robbers. Life was dangerous for peaceful people.

So the knights and barons and other lords built strong houses, usually of stone, called castles, in which they lived; and when any enemy approached, whether bears or wolves or robbers or the army of some foe, all the serfs could come into the castle and be safe, while the lord and his strong men went out to fight the enemy. So although the serfs worked hard, at least they could depend upon the lord to protect them and their wives and children; and for many years everybody thought that quite fair and the feudal system worked well enough.

But long before Columbus discovered America it had begun to break down. The serfs began to see that the lord was getting a great deal more out of it than they were; great danger arose only now and then, but work went on every day. As the country became more settled, the wild animals and the robbers were driven away. After a while things grew so quiet that the lord would not have to fight for year after year, but the serfs had to work just the same.

Towns grew up around the castles, but as the

towns grew larger the townsmen found that by putting up a wall they could take care of themselves
without the help of the lord of the castle; and they
didn't like the idea of working for him for nothing.
In many places they refused to do so, and when the
lord tried to take their goods by force they rose up
against him, killed him or drove him away, and
pulled down his castle. If the lord was a wise man,
he gave up the idea that he owned everything, and
made an agreement with the townspeople by which
they paid him taxes instead of turning over all that
they made, and the lord let them alone to manage
their own affairs. In this way the towns became free,

and little by little the serfs in the country districts became much freer than they had been. The feudal system was going to pieces.

In England it was almost completely gone by the time America was discovered. This happened for several reasons, two of them very terrible reasons — war and plague. The rule was that when a king died his oldest son, the crown prince, became king. But in England a king died who had no children, and a dispute arose over who should be king. There were two great noblemen, the Duke of Lancaster and the Duke of York, and each thought he ought to have the crown. So each called his earls and barons and

knights around him, and they fought, not once but many times. Sometimes one would gain the upper hand, sometimes the other. The dukes died, but their sons fought on, and when the sons died their grandsons continued to fight.

This went on for more than thirty years. The badge of the Duke of York was a white rose, that of the Duke of Lancaster a red rose, so the fights were called the Wars of the Roses. They were very bloody. Dukes, earls, barons, and knights were killed by dozens; frequently every man belonging to a noble family was killed, and the family disappeared. Finally, one man of the House of Lancaster, having defeated and killed the king, who was of the House of York, found that the York party had only one person left with a claim to the throne and that person was a woman. So the new king, Henry VII, married her and that ended the wars. But by that time (it was the year 1485, just seven years before Columbus made his first voyage) there were hardly any noblemen left in England. Yeomen and squires and knights had taken over the great estates and the feudal system was finished.

But it had already been weakened, fifty years before the Wars of the Roses began, by a calamity even worse than war. This was a disease that swept through all Europe, including England, which is

supposed to have killed more than half the people. A
few persons who caught this disease got well, but
most of them died within a few days. One symptom
of it was dark spots that appeared on the body
shortly before the patient died, and this made people
give it the name of the Black Death; it is supposed
to have been what doctors now call bubonic plague,
which is still found in dirty, rat-infested cities, especially in Asia.

But one effect of the Black Death in England was
to free the serfs. The reason was that so many serfs
had died that there were not enough left to work all
the land. A lord who needed a hundred serfs, and
had only two or three left, would do everything he
could to get some belonging to his neighbors. Of
course, the neighbors tried to prevent this. The result was that in order to keep his serfs from running
away, the lord had to pay them better and treat them
better. This made them somewhat like free men, and
when men get a little freedom they always want
more.

The serfs had been winning freedom all over Europe, but it seems to have happened faster in England than in most other countries. Nowhere else had
the nobility been killed off as completely as in England by the Wars of the Roses. These two facts made

Englishmen more nearly equal than were Frenchmen or Spaniards or Portuguese. To be sure, there
were still classes in England. The king was above
everybody, the dukes were above the barons, the
barons were above the knights, and the knights were
above the common people.

Yet there was a difference. In other countries,
France, for instance, nearly all the nobles had been
born noblemen, and so had their fathers and grand-
fathers and great-grandfathers before them. So
people had almost forgotten that noblemen had
ever been anything else and held the idea that there
was something special about noble blood. They
really believed that Lord So-and-so, because he was
a lord, was a different kind of animal from an ordinary man, so the ordinary people were very humble
and respectful in the presence of lords and ladies.

But by the time Henry VIII became king of England, in 1509, there were so few nobles left that
King Henry took a great many knights and made
them into barons and a great many plain men
(*commoners* was the name for them) and made
them knights. This made a great deal of new nobility
in England. Commoners were still respectful to
lords, but not quite in the same way. Old men could
remember when Lord So-and-so, or his father, had
been plain Mr. So-and-so, or at most Sir John So-

and-so, a knight not a baron. In England nobody
believed that a nobleman was a different kind of
animal from a commoner; he was just a commoner
who had done something special for the king and
had been made into a nobleman as a reward.

So the English commoners considered themselves
just about as good as anybody — not quite, though.
They admitted that if a man had done a great deed
and the king had made him a baron for it, that man
was entitled to more respect than most people. Even
if his father had done the deed, still some special
respect was due to the son who had inherited the
title. But he was not a superior being.

There was another English custom that helped
narrow the gap between commoners and noblemen.
In most of Europe all a nobleman's children were
noble, but in England only the eldest son was. All
the others became commoners unless they did something particularly fine, and so won titles of their own.
In England you frequently found a plain mister
whose brother was a lord, and a great many misters
who had uncles and cousins and nephews and nieces
among the nobility.

This is important in the history of the United
States, because it explains why the Englishmen who
came to America were so independent in spirit even
before they became independent in politics. At

home they had not been accustomed to get down on their knees before anybody. They believed, or said they believed, that God had chosen one man to be king and admitted that they ought to obey him on that account. But they didn't think God had had much to do with creating earls and barons and knights; they knew very well that King Henry VIII or his father had made most of them, and made them out of commoners.

The Englishman knew that if a lord had rights, so did a commoner. He was willing to give his lordship what was due, but he did not propose to have his own rights taken away by his lordship or anybody else — and in America by "anybody else" they meant even His Majesty the King.

But all this came up long after the time of Henry VIII. When that king died, there were no Englishmen in America, nor when his son died, nor when the daughter died who had been queen after the son's death. But then there came to the throne another daughter, who was one of the finest monarchs that England ever had. She was Elizabeth I, whom people are now beginning to call Elizabeth the Great, because it was during her reign that England became a great nation.

It is not easy to explain why this queen was great, because many things about her were not fine at all.

She was far from beautiful; she was redheaded, long-nosed, skinny, and wrinkled, but she was so vain that she loved hearing courtiers tell her how beautiful she was. She had a terrible temper, and when it burst out she would scream at people and actually slap them around in a way not at all becoming to a queen. She would not keep her promises unless it suited her, and if she thought it would help England she would tell flat lies.

All this is pretty bad, and one might think that all of it put together would make a very bad queen. But there was one good thing about Elizabeth, so important that it made up for many of her bad habits. She really loved England and worked hard to keep it safe and make it rich and strong. Other kings and queens thought of nothing but their own pleasure and despised the people except as servants to make things easy for royalty. Elizabeth was different; she might scream and throw things like a child in a tantrum when someone displeased her, but all the same she knew very well that if the English people had a duty to her, she had a duty to them, which was to keep them safe and prosperous if she could.

It was not easy; in fact, it was very hard. Elizabeth's sister Mary, who had been queen before her, had married King Philip of Spain, and when Mary died Philip felt that he ought to have the kingdom. Elizabeth had a cousin, also named Mary, who was Queen of Scotland and who had married King Francis of France. Even after Francis died the French kings felt they had a claim on Scotland, and Mary of Scotland had, after Elizabeth, the next claim on England. So Elizabeth knew that both Spain and France were ready to seize her kingdom if they could.

At the time when she became queen, England was weak. A hundred years earlier it had been strong on land, holding a large part of France from which it could summon hundreds of French knights and thousands of French men-at-arms to fight for England. A hundred years later it was to be even stronger at sea, with rich colonies and great fleets. But when Elizabeth began her reign it was in between, having lost the big army and not yet gained the big navy.

So the new queen had to be very careful what she did. Let her make one mistake, and her enemies would pounce and that would be the end of England. Fortunately for her, France and Spain hated each other, so if one threatened to make war Elizabeth could usually stop it by asking help from the other. She was like a circus acrobat walking a tightrope. As long as she kept her balance all was well, but if she leaned the least bit too far to either side she would get a bad fall.

She could not possibly conduct all the business of the kingdom herself, so she had to have wise men to help her. Now a great many men seem to be wise when they are not; to be able to tell who is really wise and who isn't is one of the most difficult things in the world, and few rulers of kingdoms have been able to do it. This is where Elizabeth proved that she was a great queen; almost every man she chose for an important job was a wise man. She didn't care in the least where she found him, if he could do the job. If the job was to fight a battle, the man must be a good soldier; if it was to govern a province, he must be a good ruler; if it was to make a treaty he must be a smart bargainer. If the man who could do the work happened to be a noble lord, all right; but Elizabeth would choose the plainest sort of commoner if he could do the work better than anyone else; and she almost always knew who could do it.

The result was that brains became very important at the court of Elizabeth. At other courts it was more important to be the son of a duke than it was to have a mind; for the sons of great lords were given important jobs whether they had any sense or not. It was not so in London. For instance, there was plain William Cecil, who had come to London as secretary to an earl, but who soon showed that he had more brains than his master. First Elizabeth chose him as

her chief adviser, then she made him a lord, and finally he became the most powerful man in the realm. She wanted to know everything that was going on in her kingdom, and William Cecil, whom she had made Lord Burleigh, was just the man to find out.

This encouraged all the smart young men in the kingdom to show what they could do, whether as soldiers, sailors, merchants, lawyers, or anything else; for if a young man did very well indeed, the queen was sure to notice him and give him an important job. If he pleased her very much, she would also give him a title and a fortune, and from that time on he would belong to the nobility.

This is the reason why Elizabeth was soon surrounded by the smartest people in England. In France and in Spain nobody could hold a high office unless he was a lord, or at least the son of a lord; and not many people could even come close enough to the king to speak to him unless they were of noble blood, or bishops or abbots or cardinals of the Roman church. But in England anybody who had done something remarkable was sent for by the queen. So every young Englishman who knew how to do anything did his best, because to do well under Elizabeth might mean fame and fortune. The result was that England became richer and stronger every day and Englishmen, even the commoners, felt that they were important.

The English sailors did best of all; for one reason, because there was so much more for them to do when Elizabeth the Great was queen. More than half the world was not yet explored, and the sailors went to work on it. Two who did especially well were Martin Frobisher and Francis Drake, for the queen made knights of both.

To us, living in the modern world, this seems odd; because a sailor who did today what Frobisher and Drake did would not be knighted, he would be hanged. They were pirates. They roamed about the seas stealing whatever they could lay their hands on that did not belong to the queen of England or to one of her good friends. Once Drake raided a Spanish colony in America and came away with a great deal of loot, including some beautiful pearls, which he gave to the queen when he got back to London, and the queen wore them in her hair at the next large party at her court.

When you hear it that way you can hardly believe that a great queen would do such a thing. That is the trouble with reading history; to understand, you must know not only what people did, but how they felt about what they were doing. Drake did not feel that he was really stealing when he took those pearls, and the queen did not feel that she was wearing stolen goods. A great poet, the greatest of all English poets, who was living at this time, wrote, "There is nothing either good or bad, but thinking makes it so." This is not entirely true, even though William Shakespeare said it, but it is true of a great many things.

To understand how Drake and the queen felt, one must remember several things. In the first place, in those days the law was what the king commanded, or what the king and some of his advisers commanded. In England for a long time it had been what the king (or queen) and Parliament decided. Parliament was the great council, divided into two parts — the nobility, from the barons up, and the commons, from the knights down. All noblemen belonged to the House of Peers, or the House of Lords, as we call it today, but members of the House of Commons were elected. A man could not be a baron without being a peer, but he could be a knight without being a member of the Commons.

However, the law extended to the edge of the kingdom, but no farther. Everyone agreed that when you crossed into the next kingdom you came under another king's law. But what about it when you did not enter another kingdom, but sailed out into the middle of the ocean, or visited some wild country where there was no proper king? Most people felt that in such places there was no law, or, rather, that every man was a law unto himself. A king who was strong enough could set up his own law wherever he went, but the subjects of other kings did not feel bound to respect it.

As for America, the English felt that the Spanish had no more right to it than they did. If the Spanish had seized whatever they could lay their hands on there — as they certainly had — why shouldn't the English seize whatever they could lay their hands on, even from the Spanish? They did, and they didn't feel the least bit guilty about it.

Behind it all was another fact. Every Englishman knew that the king of Spain claimed that he was the rightful king of England because Queen Mary had been his wife. At first he hoped to gain the kingdom without a fight, by marrying Elizabeth, but he could get no satisfaction out of her. First she said she would, and then she said she wouldn't — or, rather, she said she would and then found one excuse after another for putting off the ceremony. The truth was that she never meant to marry Philip because she didn't like him, for one thing, and for another because she did like to be queen, without having a husband to tell her what she could and could not do.

She acted so because Philip was a very powerful

king and she was afraid of him. If she made him angry enough he might try to conquer England by force. More than that, he might do it, and then he would probably chop Elizabeth's head off. So she wriggled and squirmed, and King Philip grew angrier and angrier, but not quite angry enough to go to war for a long time.

The sailors knew all this, as did everybody in England, so they felt that whatever they could do to weaken the king of Spain was done in a good cause; that is, for the safety of England. One thing that made the king of Spain strong was the gold he was getting from America, with which he could hire ships and soldiers to attack England; so to snatch his gold didn't seem stealing to the English sailors, but a grand and glorious act in defense of their country.

Such men as Frobisher and Drake became expert at that work. In their small, fast ships they could go to the West Indies and lurk among the islands (there are hundreds of them and in those days many had no people living on them) until a great Spanish treasure ship came by. Then the English would rush out and seize it.

The Spanish fought, of course, and sometimes won. They sank numbers of English ships and drowned thousands of English seamen. Often the treasure ships slipped by without being seen by the English. But the English won often enough to cut down the stream of gold and other treasure that went to Spain from Mexico and Peru.

The reason they won so often was that they depended on speed and skill, while the Spaniards relied on power. In ships of those days most of the cannon were ranged along the sides, pointing out. Only one or two guns — called bow chasers and stern chasers — pointed forward or back. Many of the Spanish galleons carried twenty guns on a side, and some carried thirty or forty. If an English ship was foolish enough to come up alongside a galleon which could fire all the guns at once — the broadside — the English ship very likely would be smashed to splinters and the fight would be over then and there.

But the English developed great skill at avoiding that. Instead, since they could usually sail faster and could always turn faster than the galleon, they would rush across in front of the galleon or behind her. That would bring the side of the English ship toward the bow or stern of the Spanish one. Then the Spaniard could fire only one or two guns, but the Englishman could fire his whole broadside, of perhaps ten or twelve. His object was to kill everybody on the decks and, if possible, shoot down the masts; if that happened, there was nothing for the Spaniard

71

to do but surrender or be shot to pieces and sunk at the Englishman's leisure.

This happened so often that the Spaniards finally had to send their treasure ships in large convoys; and even so the Englishmen, hovering about just out of range of the Spanish guns, would frequently cut out one or two ships. Then they would return to England laden with treasure, and the crowds in the streets would cheer them as heroes who had "singed the king of Spain's beard." The Spanish ambassador would protest angrily, and Queen Elizabeth would say it was all against her orders and she would do something about it. But she never did.

Finally Philip of Spain lost his temper entirely and determined to burn out this hornet's nest once for all. He spent more than two years and an immense amount of money assembling the greatest battle fleet that had ever sailed up to that time. It included one hundred and thirty ships carrying thirty thousand soldiers; and it was so much more powerful than anything that the English, or any other nation, could supply that it was called the Invincible Armada.

On paper it seemed hopeless for England as the Invincible Armada came down upon her in 1588, and the English were, in fact, horribly frightened; but they were not scared into lying down and surrendering. The queen herself spoke for them all when she said to her troops just before the battle, "I know that I have but the body of a weak and feeble woman; but I have the heart of a king, and of a king of England, too." The soldiers believed it and thought that such a queen was worth fighting for.

If sheer power had been all that counted, England would have been finished; but other things counted, too, and many of them Philip never understood. Under the Spanish system, nobody but a great lord could hold a great command; so the man chosen to lead the Armada was selected, not because he was a sailor, but because he was a duke. The poor Duke of Medina-Sidonia knew something about commanding an army, but nothing about a fleet, and he didn't want the job; but he was grander than any other nobleman available, so he had to take it. The chief officers under him were selected because they were grandees, not because they were famous fighting men.

On the other hand, the Lord High Admiral of England, Charles Howard, was also a nobleman (though a mere baron), but he had been to sea and knew something about ships. He promptly chose as his second in command, and commander of the main body of the English fleet, John Hawkins. The vanguard he gave to Martin Frobisher and the rear

guard to Francis Drake. All three had been commoners; all three had been seamen from their youth up;
and all three had distinguished themselves in sea
fights, not once but repeatedly. In gun power the
English fleet was nowhere near the Spanish, but it
was commanded by three of the best sailors that
England possessed, which meant just about the best
in the world.

The Armada appeared off Plymouth, on the south
coast of England near the end of the English Channel, and the English fleet went out to meet it there.
But the English ships did not rush in close to the
great Spanish ships, which would have blown them

out of the water. Instead, the fleet stood off and hammered the Spaniards at long range. All day the battle raged, moving slowly up the Channel. The English didn't injure the Armada seriously, but they stung it sharply. They sank one or two of the smaller ships and damaged some of the bigger ones; by night Medina-Sidonia was glad to pull into the harbor of Calais, whose forts could be trusted to make the English stand off at a respectful distance.

But Hawkins, Drake, and Frobisher knew a trick or two. They couldn't get past the forts with their larger ships, but they took a number of smaller vessels, loaded them with rosin, tar, and other inflammable stuff, set fire to them, and sent them sailing into the crowded harbor. This was too much for the Spaniards. If one of those fire ships touched a galleon it would set fire to the rigging and probably to the hull as well. The only thing to do was to get out of there, and in many cases the Spanish ships did not even wait to pull up their anchors. They simply cut the cables and fled.

Of course they rushed out of the harbor in no sort of order, and the English, waiting outside, fell on them one at a time. All the next day the battle raged, and this time the English were doing serious damage. But toward evening the wind shifted to the south, and what was left of the Armada fled northward and managed to shake off its pursuers. It must be remembered that the English had been hard hit too. Their men were very tired and most of their gunpowder had been used up. The Armada then attempted to sail around the north of Scotland and west of Ireland to get home, but it ran into one bad storm after another, and the storms finished what the English had begun. About half of the Invincible Armada finally got back to Spain, but the sea power of the Spanish had been broken, and England had suddenly become one of the world's great nations.

If you ask what this has to do with the history of the United States, the answer is that it shows what kind of people came to this country and finally won it over from all others.

They thought well of themselves — sometimes they thought too well — and after whipping Spain they didn't give a hoot for anybody. They had whipped Spain on the sea, and that gave them a great respect for sea power, so they set themselves to become better and better sailors, and soon they were the best in the world.

But, most important of all, they had learned that a man must be valued for what he can do, not for what his father did. Francis Drake's father was nobody much, but Drake was a great seaman. So was

Frobisher and so was Hawkins; these three were worth a great deal more than three men who could do nothing themselves, although their fathers might have been dukes or earls. Howard, too, was a great man, but not because he was a baron and the brother of a duke. He was great because he knew how to win a fight against an enemy bigger and stronger than he was. Incidentally, Queen Elizabeth promptly made Howard an earl, while the other three became Sir John, Sir Martin, and Sir Francis.

The first settlers brought to America this idea that every man must stand on his own two feet and not depend on his father, and it is the idea on which our whole system of government is based to this day.

Incidentally, they also brought the idea that an Englishman stands more firmly on his own feet than any other man, which was not true at all; but it helped in those early days when the going was terribly hard, and people who did not think themselves the finest men on earth might have given up and gone home.

CHAPTER THREE

The English Come to Stay

ONE REMARKABLE thing about England in the days of Elizabeth the Great was the number of Englishmen who could do many things and do them all well. For example, there was Mr. William Shakespeare, who could write a play, act a part in it, manage the theater, and at the same time be the greatest poet who ever wrote in English.

There was Judge Francis Bacon, later Sir Francis and finally Lord Verulam, who was so good a lawyer that he became chief judge of England, so good a writer that his book of essays is read to this day, and so good a philosopher that people compare him to Aristotle, the ancient Greek.

There was Sir Philip Sidney, soldier, ambassador, statesman, and also a fine poet, but remembered now as a very great gentleman. On the battlefield at Arnhem, in the Netherlands, when he was badly wounded and desperately thirsty, one of his officers brought him a cup of water; but Sidney saw a private soldier lying nearby with an even worse wound, and he made the officer give the water to the other man — something the world never forgot.

There was Robert Devereux, Earl of Essex, who fought battles, commanded fleets, courted the queen, governed Ireland, and wrote charming sonnets. But he finally plotted against Elizabeth and she had his head cut off.

Among them all, though, there was no man who could do more things, and do them well, than the Captain of the Queen's Guard, Sir Walter Raleigh. He was soldier, sailor, statesman, explorer, poet, essayist, and historian, and good at all these things; but he is of special interest to us because he made the first serious attempt to plant English settlements in America.

Walter Raleigh won his success by his brains, not by his birth. His father was a commoner, a country gentleman living in Yorkshire, and the son came to London knowing hardly anybody. The rich, proud Earl of Leicester employed a number of young gentlemen to attend him; they were called servants, but they were more like secretaries, guards, and assistants, and some of them followed the earl wherever he went. Raleigh became one of them.

There is a story that the queen first took notice of the young man when she was walking, attended by the courtiers, in the palace grounds and came to a muddy place in the path. She hesitated, not wishing to soil her shoes, and young Raleigh leaped forward, whipped off his splendid velvet cloak, and gallantly spread it over the mud so that the queen might pass dry-shod.

That story may not be true — some historians say it is not — but it is the kind of thing that would have pleased Elizabeth. She liked polite gentlemen, and she liked flattery. She would even grant favors to people who told her that she was beautiful and witty and charming (she was witty, in fact, but neither beautiful nor charming), but she never gave a man a really important job simply because he had good manners. She was too smart for that. Good manners might attract her attention in the first place, and if the polite man had brains, too, he would rise rapidly; but he had to have brains.

Raleigh had them; that, and not any velvet-cloak business, was what soon made him one of Elizabeth's great favorites. With all its brilliance of mind, the age of Elizabeth was a hard age, and this Raleigh was a hard character. He even looked a bit like a pirate. Of only medium height, he was stockily built, with broad shoulders and powerful arms that made him a first-rate swordsman. During most of his life he wore a black beard that was somewhat fierce-looking, no matter how carefully he trimmed it. He was, as they used to say long after in the American West, not bad at heart, but a very bad man to monkey with. Many people tried it, and they all regretted it, even the magnificent Earl of Essex, whom Raleigh helped convict of treason.

His ability to be very tough indeed made him the kind of man the queen needed for the tough jobs. Early in life he, with his half brother, Sir Humphrey Gilbert, had made a piratical raid on the Spaniards; later he made a startling attack on the city of Cadiz, in Spain itself, and all his life he shared in, or managed, buccaneering expeditions against the Spaniards.

All this sounds like a man whom most people would not care to meet, a rough and dangerous fellow whom peaceable men should avoid. But there was another side of Raleigh and sometimes it appeared when he was at his roughest. For instance, he was sent into Ireland, where trouble had been pretty constant ever since William the Conqueror invaded the island. Two great families, the Butlers and the Fitzgeralds, had been quarreling there for generations, and the one that happened to be getting the worst of it would always call on England for help. At this time the Butlers, whose leader was the Earl of Ormonde, were threatened by the Fitzgeralds, led by the Earl of Desmond.

Raleigh was sent over to help Ormonde, and he did it in a very big way. He went after Desmond and his crowd so furiously that when he had finished there was hardly a Fitzgerald left alive in all Ireland, and even the Butlers were rather appalled by the cruelty he showed toward the rebels. That campaign has been remembered in Ireland for three hundred years as one of the worst in Irish history.

Yet it was precisely at this time that he did two fine things, one for Ireland, the other for England. For Ireland, he introduced the potato, which his explorers had brought back from America, and which became one of the principal foods of the Irish people. For England, he discovered the poet, Edmund Spenser, living as a secretary and almost entirely neglected. Raleigh brought Spenser to London, introduced him to the queen, and persuaded her to give him wealth and honor.

Raleigh was a curious man, sometimes rough and sometimes gentle, partly pirate and partly poet, a hard fighter of all kinds of men but an equally hard student of all kinds of books, and always the bravest of the brave. He was fascinated by the tales he heard of the New World and determined that it should not all be left to Spain. He was wild to cross the Atlantic and see for himself, and he did make several voyages, but the queen did not like that at all. She was really fond of Raleigh, except when he said or did something to make her furious (he eloped with one of her maids of honor and she wouldn't speak to him for four years), and she did not wish him to drown on one of those terribly dangerous expeditions. Whenever he planned a voyage she usually found some excuse to keep him at home, so he had to do most of his exploring by sending someone else.

In 1584 he hired two sea captains, Philip Amadas and Arthur Barlowe, to explore the American coast north of the Spanish possessions in Florida. Walter Raleigh was always ready to fight if anybody chose to start a fight, but he meant this to be a peaceful expedition, which is why he told Amadas and Barlowe to stay away from the Spanish settlements. They did. Starting at what is now the coast of Georgia, they pushed on up as far as Chesapeake Bay, finding no white men anywhere, but being very much pleased with the country. Barlowe sent a report on the expedition to Raleigh. We know exactly what was in this report, because five years later a man named Richard Hakluyt included it along with many other accounts of early explorers in a book which has been reprinted many times under the title of *Hakluyt's Voyages.* It is so interesting that it is still read and may be found in many libraries.

Barlowe's report was so enthusiastic that Raleigh instantly decided that this part of the New World must be taken and held for England. He claimed everything from Florida north and, in honor of the Virgin Queen, named the whole country Virginia.

But merely claiming the country was nothing. Every king in Europe was making all sorts of claims and Spain, in particular, was claiming everything in the New World except what the Pope had given Portugal. To make a claim good it was necessary to send people over to take the land and hold it; and that was a great deal easier said than done.

To begin with, there was the matter of expense. Ships big enough and strong enough to cross the Atlantic cost a great deal of money. Besides, the sailors had to be paid and for such a long and dangerous voyage they demanded good pay. There must be food enough, not only for passengers and crew on the way over, but also to bring the crew back. Finally, the ship must carry supplies enough to keep the settlers at least a year, for it would take that long to clear land and raise a crop. It all ran to a sum that only a very rich man could afford and not many were willing to risk it, for it was doubtful that they would ever get their money back.

Raleigh was rich. Like Drake and Frobisher, he had captured a great deal of treasure from the Spaniards, and the queen had given him more; and he didn't mind spending it. In the first place, the Spaniards had proved that the New World held immense quantities of gold and silver that a bold adventurer could seize; and in the second place, Raleigh was a born adventurer and a loyal Englishman. He was the kind of man who got a thrill out of taking risks; and he was also the kind who thought that to increase the greatness of England was worth more than money. So the expense of sending out colonists did not stop him.

A harder problem was to find the kind of people who would make good colonists and who were willing to go. It is not easy for us, living nearly four hundred years later, to understand what this meant in those days. The whole world is known today. Perhaps in the ice-covered regions around the two poles it may be possible now for a man to go where nobody has gone before; but there are no longer any such places in the temperate zones and few in the tropics.

But in 1584 half the world was unknown. Amadas and Barlowe, for example, had seen and made maps of the coast of Virginia, but even they had no idea of what the country was like ten miles back from the coast. They may have sailed a few miles up a river or two, but between the rivers the trackless forest, penetrated only by a few Indian trails and the paths made by wild animals, covered everything. Most of the English believed that by traveling a few score, or maybe a few hundred, miles west one would come to what they called the South Sea and we call the Pacific. They had no idea that from the Atlantic coast it was another three thousand miles to the Pacific.

So to ask people to go and live there was asking them to go and live on the extreme edge of nowhere. Not many liked the idea, and those who did were mostly wild, harum-scarum fellows willing to go anywhere and dare anything, but not much good as steady workmen who would build houses and plant crops and raise families. But steady workmen were needed for a new colony.

It took Raleigh a long time to find them. He tried twice, first with a group of men whom he sent over in 1585, but they were not equal to the task. Ten months later, when Francis Drake happened by on one of his voyages, they were on the verge of starvation and so discouraged that he loaded them all on board and took them home. Two years later Raleigh tried again, this time with a group including women and children as well as men, under the leadership of John White as governor. This seemed a good idea, as White had been there before; he had gone out with the expedition of 1585 as a sort of scientific observer. He was a good artist and his job was to make pictures of the plants, animals, and Indians of the region. He came back with sixty-three water colors, which are the only pictures we have of how the country looked when the first white men came.

They had chosen what they thought was an ideal spot for a settlement. Off the coast of that part of Virginia that is now North Carolina lies a chain of sand bars, not continuous, but broken by a few inlets deep enough for the ships of those days to pass through. Behind them, protected by the bars, lies a stretch of smooth water, thirty miles wide in some places. At a spot where the sound is only six or seven miles across, is an island twelve miles long and three or four wide, rising thirty or forty feet above the water level. The Indians called it Roanoke.

Roanoke Island had several advantages in the eyes of the explorers. Ships could ride at anchor near it, sheltered by the sand banks from the storms of the Atlantic. The same banks also made it fairly safe from any raiding Spaniard, for a ship could approach it only through the inlets, which had narrow, twisting channels that were easy to guard. On the other side, several miles of water separated it from the mainland and any hostile Indians who might be there. They could reach Roanoke only by canoe. At the same time, the island was big enough to support a fairly large settlement.

The place itself was beautiful — covered with great trees, pine, live oak, dogwood, magnolia, and many others. In the forest were tangled vines of wild grapes, the spicy muscadine, whose fragrance was carried on the breeze across miles of water. Among them was a single vine of a white muscadine found nowhere else in the world, and later called the scuppernong.

To people reaching Roanoke after many weeks at sea it seemed a heavenly place; and yet it was a death trap.

John White had many good qualities, but not the one quality that he needed most. He was a careful observer, an excellent artist, and a brave man, but his judgment was poor. He was the leader; therefore his place was with the colonists. He was the one man with practical experience, since he had been to Roanoke before, which was another reason for his sticking to the colonists.

Nevertheless, as soon as the colonists had erected a few houses protected with earthworks and a palisade, which they called Fort Raleigh, it became plain that they would need a great many more sup-

plies than they had brought with them. White should have sent for them, but instead he determined to go back and get them himself.

He did not mean to desert. Nobody thinks that. But a great many people think he was a rattlebrained fellow, always dashing off after the latest idea that crossed his mind, forgetting more important things. He had one very strong reason for taking care of Roanoke Island: his daughter was there. Eleanor White had married a colonist named Ananias Dare. While they were getting settled on the island their first child was born, and they named the baby girl after the country, Virginia. She was the first child of English-speaking parents born in what is now the United States.

Nine days after the birth of Virginia Dare her grandfather, Governor John White, sailed for England — and no white man ever set eyes on any of the colonists again.

When White reached England he found everything in a turmoil. It was known that the Spanish Armada was getting ready to sail, and the government was seizing every ship and every man available to defend the country. Sending a ship to Roanoke was not to be thought of when England itself might be invaded any day. John White had to stay until the danger should be over.

Then the Spaniards delayed and delayed. Months passed before the Armada made any move at all. Other months passed while it came slowly up from the south, stopping here and there to take on more men or to pick up additional ships. More than a year passed before the enemy fleet came in sight and the battle began. Then the days stretched into weeks while the fight raged up the English Channel, into the North Sea, around the north end of Scotland, and down the west coast of Ireland. It is true that the really big fighting was over within the first week, but the long pursuit that followed scattered the English, as well as the Spanish, over a wide area.

Then it was necessary to collect the ships, clean up the wreckage, straighten things out, and make sure that the Spaniards had really had enough. All this took a great deal of time, for things moved much more slowly in those days when ships depended on the wind and there was no such thing as radio to find out where they were.

Altogether, it was more than two years before England felt that she could afford a ship to take Governor White back to his colony. When he finally reached Roanoke, it was to find Fort Raleigh deserted. There was no sign of a fight. The fort was not damaged, except by wind and weather. Apparently the colonists had left it of their own accord, but there was no indication of where they had gone except the word *Crotoan* carved on the trunk of one tree and the letters C R O with a cross on another. The word, later spelled *Croatan,* meant either a place or an Indian tribe, somewhere vaguely to the south. White never found it, for one reason because the stormy season was coming on and the captain of his ship wanted to get away from that dangerous coast before a hurricane struck it. They did look around a little, but not very much, and then went back to England. The colony had vanished forever into the vast, unknown continent lying to the west.

Hundreds of years later, when scholars began to collect sketches of famous Americans into the many

volumes that are called the *Dictionary of American Biography* they included an article twenty lines long on Virginia Dare. As she is not known to have lived longer than nine days, she is the youngest person given a separate article in the *Dictionary*, and probably the youngest so mentioned in any similar work.

That was Raleigh's last effort to plant a colony in America. He was always interested, always planning to try again, but the opportunity never came. Twelve years later the great queen died and was succeeded by the biggest fool that ever sat on the throne of England. This was James, King of Scotland, and son of that Queen Mary whom Elizabeth had beheaded. James (called the Sixth in Scotland, but the First in England) was the kind of man who could believe any kind of lie but could seldom recognize the truth when he heard it. Raleigh's enemies, led, of course, by the Spanish ambassador, immediately surrounded the king and poured into his ears all sorts of stories against Raleigh. Some of them no doubt were true, but the one that impressed the king was false from the ground up. It was the lie that said Raleigh was a traitor to his country. On that charge Raleigh was arrested, imprisoned in the Tower of London for thirteen years, and at last beheaded.

But Raleigh was Raleigh to the last. In prison, with a death sentence hanging over him, never knowing on what day he might go to the block, he spent his time writing a history of the world; and on the scaffold he examined the headsman's axe and remarked, "Sharp medicine, but it cures all diseases." This was the man who was first among the founders of our country, and his example encouraged those who came after him and succeeded. He had his faults, but none can deny that he was a manful man whom we can remember with pride.

There is nothing to boast about in the fact that the English got their start in America under James I, rather than under the great Elizabeth and her man Raleigh. But there is nothing really unusual in it. It often happens, especially when something new is being tried, that a great man works long and hard, and fails. Then some smaller man comes along and succeeds easily. What has happened is that the great man has opened the way, which was the harder part of the work, and the small man then comes in and, by doing the easier part, gets credit for the whole.

As a matter of fact, King James did nothing much for America, except in a sort of left-handed way. He treated one group of his people so badly that they left England and went to America, choosing to risk living among the wolves and the Indians rather than under such a king. Since they happened to be very smart people indeed, their coming helped America; but it was no thanks to the king.

What he did do was to grant permission to some businessmen to make an effort to take over the new land at their own expense; and even in this James took very good care of himself. If the businessmen lost everything, why, that was no concern of his; but if they found any gold or silver, James was to have one fifth of it.

This looks like a pretty bad deal for the businessmen, and so in fact it was; but when James I was king of England, the Englishmen really had very few rights, and James was doing his best to take away those few. His son, Charles I, did the same thing, which is why the English people at last rose up, took Charles from the throne, cut off his head, and did without a king for eleven years. But that happened after the settlement of America was already well started.

The businessmen of those days didn't think the deal was too bad. They had great confidence in themselves and more confidence in England. They knew that Spain had done wonderfully well in the New World and, especially after beating the Armada, they felt that anything a Spaniard could do, an Englishman could do twice as well. They were wrong. The Englishman may have been better as a sailor; but on land the Spaniard, as an explorer, was twice as good as the Englishman any day. Before the English even started for North America the Spaniards were already all over Mexico, halfway up the Pacific coast and up the Atlantic coast from the tip of Florida almost as far as Savannah, in what is now the State of Georgia. The oldest city in the United States today is one that the Spaniards founded forty-two years before the English could make a settlement that lasted. It is St. Augustine, in Florida, established in 1565, when Walter Raleigh was a boy of thirteen.

However, as long as the English believed they could outdo the Spaniards they were willing to try. In fact, they made a double try. Two groups of businessmen applied to the king for permission to make settlements in Virginia. Each group called itself "The Virginia Company," but since one was located at London and the other at Plymouth, most people called them "The London Company" and "The Plymouth Company." The king issued a written permit, called a charter, to each company, but to prevent their fighting among themselves he decreed that the London Company should plant its first colony somewhere between 34 degrees and 38 degrees north latitude, while the Plymouth Company should take a spot between 41 degrees and 45 degrees. The land between, from latitude 38 to 41, might be settled by either.

The thirty-fourth parallel of latitude touches the Atlantic coast at the mouth of the Cape Fear River in North Carolina; the thirty-eighth crosses the mouth of the Potomac River where it empties into Chesapeake Bay. So the London Company could settle anywhere between the Cape Fear and the Potomac. The forty-first parallel runs through Long Island Sound and touches the mainland at Port Chester, just above New York City; the forty-fifth touches the coast in Nova Scotia, now a part of Canada. So the Plymouth Company could settle anywhere between New York and Nova Scotia.

Of course, the king of England had no more right to this land than the king of Spain or the king of France or any other king. If anybody had a right to the land, it was the Indians who lived on it. But in those days nobody assumed that naked savages had any rights. In fact, no man had any rights of his own, but only such as were given him. For many centuries everybody in Europe had believed that the only rights an ordinary man possessed were those he got from the king; and the king, in turn, got his rights from God.

Naturally, if the king worshipped a false god, he couldn't get anything but false rights, nor could he give his subjects any real rights. In Christian Europe it was assumed that the Mohammedans worshipped a false god, Mohammed, so the Turks and Arabs and Moors had no rights that a Christian was bound to respect. It did no good for the Turks and the rest to point out that they did not regard Mohammed as a god, but only as the prophet of the same God that the Jews and the Christians worshipped. The Christians continued to regard them as infidels who had no rights.

Then the Christians split up among themselves. Some of them continued to follow the Pope at Rome, others the Patriarch at Constantinople, and still others Martin Luther in Germany, John Calvin in France, and Henry VIII in England. Each denied that the rest had any God-given rights, so each felt perfectly justified in taking what he could from those who followed a different faith. They fought among themselves for more than a hundred years in what came to be known as the Wars of Religion. Nobody could win, and among them they almost destroyed Europe; so at last they quit fighting, but they did not quit hating each other and denying each other's rights.

This was the situation when America was discovered. No nation would admit that any other nation had a right to the new land. The one thing they could agree on was that the Indians could not possibly have any real right to it, because the Indians had never even heard of the Christian, the Jewish, or the Mohammedan God and could not have acquired any rights from him.

Sir Robert Cecil, chief man in the London Company, and Sir John Popham, leader of the Plymouth Company, meant to take the land away from both the Indians and the Spaniards if they could, but it did not seem to them that they were robbing anybody. They thought of themselves as very honest men, because they meant to stay away from any place that the Spaniards had already settled. Sir Robert's people could not go south of Cape Fear, and the whole width of what is now South Carolina lay between Cape Fear and the most northern Spanish settlement. If they stayed two hundred miles away from the Spaniards, wasn't that fair enough?

All this may not seem very important now, but it is important because it explains a great deal about America. If you do not know the ideas that the first Americans had, what they did will look very strange. Some things will look silly and others will look wicked, when they really were neither silly nor wicked but simply mistaken.

Many times in the story of America you will find good men doing things that had terrible effects; yet the men meant well, so how can you blame them? What makes a man bad is not doing what is wrong, but doing what he knows is wrong.

What we need most of all is to know what we are doing. This is so important that thousands of years ago one of the greatest of men, Socrates, decided that the only really good thing in the world is knowledge. Today most people do not agree. They think that there are other good things, but they have to admit that Socrates was partly right, because without knowledge a man often does evil when he wants to do good. So if one wants to be a good American it is necessary to know how America began, and how

it has gone on since, and why it has gone the way it has and not some other way.

When Sir Robert Cecil got together a group of men who were willing to go and live in Virginia, taking the land from the Indians and keeping it from the Spaniards, he had no idea that he was preparing to rob anybody. He was sure that the Indians would be better off if they were ruled by the English king and taught to be Protestant Christians than if they fell under the Spanish king and were taught to be Catholic Christians. Whether he was right or wrong is not the point; he thought that instead of robbing the Indians he was giving them something of great

value, including the possibility of going to heaven when they died, and he had no doubt that he was acting as a civilized gentleman and a true Christian ought to act.

So he assembled a hundred and five bold fellows and started them out in December, 1606, under the command of a sea captain named Christopher Newport, who had a reputation as a daring and skillful explorer. It took them four months, not to cross the Atlantic, but to explore the coast looking for a good place to found a colony. At last, in April, 1607, they came to a huge estuary emptying into the sea between two capes, which they named for the king's sons, Cape Charles and Cape Henry. Sailing between the capes they found a bay extending forty miles to the west and two hundred miles to the north. Six great rivers entered this bay. They chose the one farthest south, which they named for the king himself, James; and thirty-two miles from the river's mouth they landed on a peninsula, built a palisade of logs across the narrow neck of the peninsula, and behind the palisade erected rude shelters. They named the place Jamestown and it was the first permanent English settlement in what is now the United States.

CHAPTER FOUR

Village in the Wilderness

THE JAMES, where it passes Jamestown, is a mighty river. It is about two miles across and so deep that large ocean-going ships can come up that far without touching bottom. In 1607, of course, ships were much smaller and the biggest in the world at that time could easily come to Jamestown.

But in 1607 it was also a lonely river. Until Newport's ships arrived it had never seen a sail or any kind of boat larger than Indian dugouts, and it did not see many of those. In the twentieth century it is not possible for men to know the kind of loneliness that the early settlers in this country felt, because it is not possible to get as far away from all other people as they were. The loneliest places in the world today are the North and South Poles; but when Admiral Byrd went to the South Pole he kept in touch by radio with his base camp, and the base camp was in touch with New York. If anything had happened to Byrd the world would have known it in a few minutes; but what happened in Jamestown could not possibly be known in England for many months.

This had an effect on the spirits of the settlers. We can see that plainly, but it is not easy for us to understand how great was the effect, simply because we have never known such great loneliness. None but brave men started on that trip, and even brave men found the situation pretty hard to take after Captain Newport had landed the colonists and then had gone back for more. The voyage across the Atlantic was as dangerous as it was slow; the settlers had no assurance that Newport would ever get to England, or if he got there that he would ever get back. Yet everything depended on his return with more people and more supplies. When many months had passed and the time when he might get back was getting close, they kept a man on watch down at the mouth of the river; and when at last he spied the sails, and came tearing to the village to tell the people that the captain was coming, they were so joyful that they gave a special name to the spot where the watchman stood. There is a large city on that spot today, but it is still known as Newport News.

Worse than the loneliness was the strangeness of

the country. There was nothing like it in England —
no river like the mighty James, no forest like the
enormous pines that covered its banks, no animals
like the raccoon and the opossum, or birds like the
wild turkeys and parakeets, no plants like the maize
and the potato that the Indians had cultivated;
above all, no people like the Indians themselves.
The Englishmen didn't know which plants and animals were good to eat and which were unfit for food.
They didn't know which snakes were poisonous and
which harmless, nor where were the best places to
fish. They didn't know anything about the country
itself, or what it could produce.

There was no such heat in England as oppressed
them in a Virginia summer, no such thunderstorms
as crashed and roared over their heads, no such hurricanes as lashed the land in spring and autumn.
Everything was strange and many things were gigantic by comparison with what they had known —
the trees, the rivers, the storms, the distances. It was
a vast and terrifying land.

The Indians, roaming through the forest, or coming down the river in their boats made of hollowed-
out logs (these Indians did not have the light canoes
made of birch bark found farther north), watched
the white men at first with more curiosity than fear.
There seemed nothing to be afraid of on that spit of

land sticking out into the river with its little huddle of houses behind a log palisade cutting it off from the forest.

The white men had strange ways, most of which seemed foolish ways to the Indians, and some of them *were* foolish. For one thing, they insisted on wearing heavy clothes and clumsy shoes or long boots in the hottest weather, when the Indian found a loincloth and a pair of moccasins made of deer hide quite enough. When they traveled any distance they added to their clothes steel armor, or at least a helmet and corselet of steel.

They also did a great deal more work than the Indians thought necessary in building their houses.

The Indians built theirs by taking slender green poles, sticking them in the ground in rows, and weaving them together with vines or withes to make walls a few feet apart. Then they would bend the tops of the poles toward each other until they met and could be tied together with vines, making an arched roof, which they would cover with bark or thatch or anything that would shed water.

Just how the first houses in Jamestown were built we do not know, but we do know that they were not log cabins. It seems strange, but it is true that with millions of trees all around them neither the Indians nor the English settlers ever thought of a log cabin. Not until thirty years later, when the Swedes settled on the Delaware, was the first log cabin built in this country.

Probably the first houses in Jamestown were built after the fashion used in England for laborers' cottages. First, round logs were flattened on four sides with axes and laid on the ground to form a square, fastened at the corners with wooden pins driven into holes bored with augers. Then lighter pieces were raised on end at the corners, and still lighter ones laid across the tops of the uprights, all being fastened together with wooden pins. Between the corner pieces other light uprights, called studding, were placed, sometimes with cross braces, horizontal or at an angle. Finally, the open spaces were filled with a mixture of mud and straw packed in as tightly as possible. The roof was made of rafters covered with thatch, or sometimes overlapping pieces of bark which shed rain water.

It all sounds very flimsy, but it really isn't. As long as the top of the wall is kept dry such houses are durable. There are some in England that have stood for hundreds of years, and the mud walls are warm in winter and cool in summer. There were probably no windows in the first houses and the floors were of earth packed hard. Chimneys — when they had any except a hole in the roof to let the smoke out — were built of mud held together with sticks, the coating of mud on the inside being extra thick to keep the sticks from burning.

The Indians couldn't see the sense in all this labor, for it was never the habit of the Indians to build permanent towns. They would settle in one place long enough to raise a crop of corn and some beans and squash, but what they really depended on was hunting, and they had to be ready to move to where the game was most plentiful. It would have been foolish for them to work hard at building strong houses that they would use for no more than a few months.

Still, if the white men wanted to do it, the Indians

at first saw no reason to object, and for some time white men and red men in Virginia got along very well. On several occasions the Indians made presents to the whites of such things as deer, wild turkeys, corn, and other food, and the whites returned such things as knives, hatchets, mirrors, and beads. Later the Indians were usually willing to sell food and skins and other forest products.

At first the great danger to the Jamestown settlers was not the Indians but the land itself and their own ignorance and folly. In a country they knew nothing about they were always making mistakes, and some of them were the kind of mistakes that a man doesn't make more than once. For instance, a man who had never seen or heard of a rattlesnake or a moccasin (the snake, not the shoe) might not move fast when he first came upon one, or might even pick it up. No man made that mistake twice, because he wouldn't be alive to make it; or if he lived, as a good many did even after being bitten, he would have been so very sick for so long a time, that nothing would induce him to go near a snake again.

Of the one hundred and five people that Christopher Newport brought to Jamestown, seventy-three were dead in less than a year. This is a terrible death rate and in our mild, safe country we are likely to

think that there simply wasn't any excuse for it. But if we think a little longer we can see that it really was not at all astonishing. Perhaps the new land could not have been taken over in any other way. Our country wasn't made as mild and safe as it is now by any easy means. To say nothing of the wars that had to be fought, just the work of making the country fit to live in was a terrible job, and more brave men than we can count were killed in doing it. When we remember that, we think more highly of the country than we would if we believed that it had always been easy and pleasant.

To begin with, the kind of men who came to Virginia in 1607 were not careful men. If they had been, they would have stayed at home. Most of them were wild, reckless fellows who loved excitement more than they feared danger. They had all heard stories of Mexico and Peru. They had heard that men who went as private soldiers with Cortes and Pizarro, men who hadn't two pennies to chink together when they left, had come back to Spain after a few years loaded with gold and pearls and jewels, with which they had bought fine houses and thereafter lived like rich men. If it could happen to Spaniards in Mexico and Peru, why couldn't it happen to Englishmen in Virginia?

Of course, the answer was that most of the gold in

North America was on the other side of the continent, thousands of miles from Virginia. But nobody knew that. Most of the men who came to Jamestown with that first group expected to find rich mines without much trouble and they wasted a great deal of time looking for them when they should have been at work clearing the forest and planting seed so as to be sure of having something to eat when winter came. But no, they must be looking for gold, and there was great excitement when they found a kind of clay filled with bright yellow specks that looked like gold. It was not. It was only what they called in England "fool's gold," because it fooled so many people into believing it was the real thing. The scientific name for it is iron pyrites, and it is quite common; but the settlers dug up a great quantity of it and loaded it into Newport's ships when he started back to England.

But there were a few among them who were not so foolish. These men understood that the important thing was not the discovery of gold but possession of the land itself. The London Company had sent sealed orders, not to be opened until the landing, regarding the management of the colony. When they were opened it appeared that things were to be run by a council of seven men, of whom Newport was one. But among the other six was a man who was already under arrest on account of a row he had had with some of the ship's officers on the voyage. For a month they would not allow him to sit in the council, so he took a small boat and began to explore the country. This was the famous Captain John Smith, who in the end did more than any other one man to bring about English possession of America.

The men who had to work with him would never have believed it, for he really was a very tough character — loudmouthed, boastful, hard to get along with, and, as some of them felt sure, the biggest liar in the New World. The story of his life, as he told it, is pretty hard to believe, and for a long time historians refused to accept it; but part of it is certainly true, and about the rest we simply don't know.

It is true that Smith was born into a fairly good family, that he attended a good grammar school but not a university, and that he inherited a little money from his father. It is true that he refused to go into his father's business, but instead went abroad and became a soldier. Apparently he didn't care much on which side of a war he fought; he served first in one army, then in another. It seems to be true that he got into eastern Europe, where there was incessant war with the Turks. For all that we have some proof outside of what he said.

But then begins the fancy part, about which we

know nothing except what John Smith told us. At the time when war against the Turks was being waged by a great Hungarian prince named Sigismund Bathory, John Smith said that he joined the Hungarian army and became a favorite of the prince. He said that on one occasion when the two armies were facing each other, three gigantic Turks rode out into the no man's land between them and offered to fight any three men in the Hungarian army. He said that he alone went out to accept the challenge, fought the Turks one after another, and killed all three, which so pleased the prince that he gave Smith a coat of arms bearing a picture of three Turks' heads. He did claim a coat of arms with three Turks' heads, but whether Prince Sigismund gave it to him or he just decided on it for himself, nobody knows.

He said later he was wounded in battle and captured, sent to Constantinople, made a slave, and presented to the pasha's wife, who had the astonishing name of Tragabigzanda; but she fell in love with him and sent him away to her brother, who ruled a province in the interior of Turkey. After a time John Smith, once more a slave, killed his master, and after many hair-raising adventures got back to England, where he helped organize the London Company and so came to Jamestown.

Because there is no proof of all this, many people

have believed that John Smith made up the whole story, and perhaps he did. On the other hand, if it all really happened there would be no proof, for in those days and in that part of the world people kept records only of the most important events, and a great many of those that were kept were lost in the incessant battles and sieges and burning of towns that went on for centuries. The fact is, we just don't know.

What we do know is that he was very strong, very active, and very hard to kill. His mind was as active as his body. When he went exploring he did not merely look and come away; he took surveying instruments, made measurements, and drew maps that were remarkably accurate, considering what poor instruments he had. He made note of rivers, islands, and bays; he carefully examined plants and animals; he wrote down the nature of the soil in different places. In 1608 he took a barge, a large rowboat with twelve oarsmen, and went from Jamestown clear up the Chesapeake Bay, looking into the creeks and rivers and finding good places for future settlements. At what is now Baltimore he found a high hill of dark red clay and called the place Bolus, because the hill reminded him of *bole armoniac,* or rouge. All this information he sent back to England.

But what impressed people most at the time was

the way he handled things at Jamestown. A good deal that was going on there — for instance, all that rushing around looking for gold, when the colonists should have been making sure of something to eat — he didn't like at all, and he said so, loudly and frequently. This angered the other members of the council, and they talked back. One quarrel followed another, but after Newport had left for England, and things began to get worse and worse, many of the settlers began to see that John Smith was right and to take his part. Once, though, they came very near hanging him, and would have done so had not Newport come back at that moment, bringing new settlers and more supplies; he listened to both sides of the argument and at the end, instead of hanging Smith, made him governor.

Two stories about him have always been remembered. The settlers included all kinds of people, among them some who called themselves gentlemen and fancied that they were too good to work in the fields like common laborers, even though it was plain that unless everybody worked to raise food they were all going to starve. When they reported to Governor Smith that the gentlemen were refusing to hoe corn, he issued a rule that Americans ever since have regarded as rough but fair. He said, "He that will not work neither shall he eat." They knew that he would enforce it, too, so the gentlemen thereafter went out with the rest.

The other is one of his own yarns, which may or may not be true. The Indians were divided into small tribes, each with its chief; but over them all was a sort of chief of chiefs, named Powhatan. Once when food in Jamestown was very scarce John Smith went to Powhatan's camp to try to buy or beg corn to tide the settlers over. But for some reason Powhatan was in a bad mood at the time, so instead of giving the white men anything, he ordered his warriors to seize them and tie them up while he decided what to do with them. His mood must have been very bad, for after some time he decided to finish

them off, or at least the leader, Smith. So the warriors threw him to the ground and put his head on a stump, and then one of them picked up a big club, intending to smash his skull. But at that moment Powhatan's little twelve-year-old daughter ran out and threw herself on Smith so that the men couldn't strike without hitting the princess, who begged her father for his life. The child, Pocahontas, was Powhatan's favorite, so after a little hesitation, he ordered the executioners to let the white man live, and soon afterward released him.

Here, again, we have only Smith's word for it, and some people think he made up the story many years later. But we do know that such things sometimes happened among the Indians. If a woman took a fancy to a prisoner she might ask the chief for him and the chief might agree. So it could have happened just as Smith said it did.

Anyhow, we know that there was an Indian princess named Pocahontas, because years later she married an Englishman, John Rolfe, who took her to London, where the king and queen made much of her. She died in England but left a son who, when he grew up, came to Virginia and became a rich man. Many of his descendants are living in Virginia still.

But the best work that Captain John Smith did for America was not done in Virginia. Before he went back to England he made a voyage to the northern part of the land. Later he drew maps of the coast so carefully and accurately that ship captains could use them as guides. It was all Virginia then, but to this northern part of it he gave a special name — New England. Soon everybody was in the habit of dividing America into two parts, Virginia and New England.

What the new country needed above all else was more people, and John Smith did more to bring people to it than any other one man. He could do it because he was, among other things, a writer. Even before he left Jamestown he had written one small book praising the country, telling what it was like and explaining that it was a fine place to live. Captain Newport took it back to England and the company had it printed to advertise the new land. In those days they gave long titles to books, and the spelling was very different from ours. The title of Smith's first book was *A True Relation of Such Occurrences and Accidents of Noate as Hath Hapned in Virginia since the First Planting of That Collony.*

Later Smith wrote a great many other books and pamphlets, all meant to induce people to go and settle in America. There is no doubt that he skipped over a good many of the bad features and made life in America seem easier than it really was. But in general he told the truth, and from him thousands of people learned more about America than they had learned from anyone else. It seems certain that a great many of those who went there to live were persuaded to go by John Smith.

If the king of Spain or the king of France paid any attention at all to Jamestown for the first ten or fifteen years after its founding they did not give it much. It certainly did not seem to offer any threat to their great empires, still less a threat to the very idea of kings and kingship. How could one tiny village, set down on the edge of a wilderness that, as far as anyone knew then, had no end, be a threat to the mighty nations of Europe? If the kings thought about it at all, which they probably did not, they would have laughed at the suggestion that this place was a danger to them.

Yet a person who looks at it closely can see in Jamestown the promise of many of the things that made America what it is today. It was like an acorn planted last year. This year it is a little sprout, two or three inches high, with a pair of leaves. It is very frail; with your thumb and forefinger you can pull it out of the ground; you can step on it and crush it to death. Yet all the same it has roots, trunk, and leaves, which are the three things necessary to the life of a huge oak that can bear tremendous weights and stand up against hurricanes.

In Jamestown were many of the things that made the United States not only strong but also different from the nations of Europe. In part it was what the settlers did, but in very large part it was their ideas, the way they thought. For instance, there was John Smith's rule, "He that will not work, neither shall he eat." That wasn't the rule in England or anywhere else in Europe. As far back as anyone could remember there had always been nobility and gentry who were allowed to eat and to eat very well indeed, although they did no work. Even in Jamestown, at first, nobody saw anything wrong with that system. But in the new land there simply wouldn't be enough to eat unless everybody worked. Back in Europe the gentlemen had to do the fighting to protect those who were doing the work; but in America when the Indians turned hostile everybody had to do the fighting. When farmers went to hoe in the cornfield, they took a gun along and kept it close by so that they could snatch it up the instant a savage appeared. So if workers had to help with the fighting, why shouldn't gentlemen help with the work? The more they thought about it, the more Americans became convinced that John Smith's rule was a good one.

Little by little we learned more about farming and invented better tools, so the time passed long ago when it was necessary for everybody to work on the land in order to produce enough food. But the idea remained in people's minds. To this day most Americans think that a man should do something if he is going to claim the right to eat. It is no longer necessary for him to hoe corn, but he should do something — perhaps study how to raise better corn, or to build better houses, or to govern the country more fairly, or to understand and help others understand all the things that worry and perplex us. All this is work,

just as much as hoeing in a cornfield, and workers at these things are needed even more than men to hoe. But the principle is the same. An American gentleman should work at something, or he has no excuse to be here at all.

This doesn't mean that he has to work for money. A great deal of the hardest and finest work in the country is done for very little money, or none at all. But it adds something to the country. That is the point. A man who adds something to the country, whether he is paid or unpaid, has a right to live here; a man who adds nothing is allowed to live

here, but a great many Americans doubt that he has any real right to do so, and they have little respect for him.

Another idea that showed up early at Jamestown and that Americans have clung to ever since is that the man on the spot knows better what to do than the man at a distance, even though the man far away may be a very smart fellow.

When the London Company got over the delusion that there were great quantities of gold in Virginia, they realized that the next best thing they could get from the new country was wood. England was already beginning to be a great trading nation, and to supply her trade she trained skilled workmen to make vast quantities of things, especially woolen cloth and things made of metal. But to melt and work metal she needed charcoal, which is partly burned wood; and to finish and dye her cloth she needed potash, which came from wood ashes. Then to carry her goods she needed ships, which were built of wood; and of course she needed lumber for houses and furniture and wagons and countless other things.

But by 1607 England had cut down most of her own forests and was bringing in wood from Sweden and Russia and other countries, which was not a good idea, because in case of war these other countries could and would cut off the supply. In America the forests seemed to have no end, so the London Company decided that what they needed from the colony was wood, and the products that came from wood: tar, rosin, tanbark, potash, and many others.

They could also use ore, especially iron ore, or, even better, the iron itself. The system was for the colonists to dig the ore, then burn charcoal, and with the charcoal smelt out the iron and send it to England. There the English workmen would make it into knives, tools of all kinds, and machines. That is to say, America was to supply England with raw materials from which the English would make all sorts of valuable things, from ships to penknives, which they could sell profitably all over the world.

This sounded fine on paper, and it was fine for England, but it wasn't so good for the colonists. There is a great deal of labor but not much profit in producing raw materials. The big profit is in turning out a finished product; but at first there seemed to be no valuable product that could be finished in Virginia.

Then John Rolfe, the Englishman who married Pocahontas, discovered one. The Spaniards had brought tobacco to Europe from the West Indies, and it was increasingly popular.

Sir Walter Raleigh is said to have introduced it

into England, and there are two curious stories about Raleigh and tobacco. It is said that he had just lighted his pipe one day when in came a servant who had never seen anyone smoking; the servant was bringing a tankard of ale and, seeing smoke issue from Sir Walter's mouth, thought he was on fire and threw the ale all over him. The other is that he once made a bet with Queen Elizabeth that he could weigh the smoke from a pipeful of tobacco. He poured out a little tobacco, weighed it, put it in his pipe and smoked it, then knocked out the ash, weighed it, and subtracted the weight of the ash from the weight of the tobacco, which told him the weight of the smoke. The queen laughed and paid up.

The demand for tobacco in England was great and was increasing. The Indians in Virginia grew tobacco, but it was poor stuff, weak and flavorless. But Rolfe found that by carefully cultivating Virginia tobacco, cutting it when it was just beginning to ripen, and curing it under shelter instead of leaving it to dry in the sun, he could produce a tobacco as good as the Spanish.

He sent some to England, where it was snapped up at a good price; so then he started cultivating it in a big way. The other colonists followed his example, and soon they found that they could make six times as much out of tobacco as they could out of anything else. So everybody started raising tobacco very much as everybody had gone hunting gold in the first year; at one time they were actually growing tobacco in the streets of Jamestown.

This didn't please the London Company any too well, but there was not much they could do about it. It took labor to raise tobacco, but it also took labor to fell trees and dig iron ore and burn charcoal; and labor in Virginia was very expensive. So the colonists were determined to use what labor they had on the thing that would bring in most money, which was tobacco. In London they meant well but they just couldn't understand the way things were in Virginia; only the people who were there really understood what ought to be done.

Here are two ideas that started in Jamestown but spread through the whole country and are recognized as American ideas to this day. One is that you can't stand off hundreds or thousands of miles and tell the man on the job how to do his work. In everything else you may be much smarter, but when it comes to the job he has on hand he knows more about it than you can know; so it is best to let him do it his own way, or at least to listen carefully to what he has to say about it.

The other idea is so simple that it seems to us that

everyone ought to understand it, yet it is very decidedly American. It is this: if you can't make a living at what you are doing, do something else. No matter if the other thing is something you have never done before, go ahead and try it. You can't do worse and you may do better.

We don't know what John Rolfe had in mind when he came to Virginia, but it certainly wasn't raising tobacco. Tobacco wasn't grown in England so he couldn't have known anything about it. In England he rated as a gentleman, so it seems likely that what he intended to do was get a lot of land, hire laborers to work it, and live on what they made. But when he got here he found that it couldn't be done. It was easy enough to get land, but there simply weren't any laborers, or not nearly enough to till a large estate. He couldn't make a living in the way he intended, so he looked about for something else. His discovery of how to produce fine tobacco made not only his own fortune but that of the whole colony.

In the twentieth century we are likely to say to ourselves, well, what is remarkable about that? Anyone with good sense would have done the same. But when we say that, we forget how people in Europe thought in 1607 and how people in many parts of the world still think. For centuries any man who changed his job was regarded as a queer fellow, and sometimes as a criminal. If a man's father had been a farmer, the man was supposed to be a farmer; if the father had been a shoemaker, the son was supposed to be a shoemaker, and so on. Even today in most European countries it is hard for a man who has worked for years at one job to change to another — not as hard as it used to be, but much harder than it is in America.

Here it is not unusual for a young man to try two or three, or perhaps five or six different jobs before he finds the thing that he can do best. We think nothing of it, but it astonishes people from other countries and gives some of them the notion that Americans are a very fickle people, never knowing what they want. The truth is, it has been our way of acting ever since Jamestown, not because we chose to act in that way, but because in the beginning we had to, and we found that it worked very well. So we have acted that way ever since.

However, the most important thing that we can trace back to Jamestown started a dozen years after the colony was founded. By that time settlements had spread in many directions. When it was found that you could really make money raising tobacco, many more people were willing to come to the new country, and a different kind of people. When it was all an adventure that people thought of as consisting mostly, of fighting savages and hunting for treasure, careful, steady, hard-working men didn't think much of it, and only the wild, harum-scarum fellows liked it. But when it was learned that by steady work in the tobacco fields a man could make several times as much in the colony as he could hope to make in England, then law-abiding, reliable men — fathers of families — began to see reason in going abroad.

So the London Company was able to send people across the Atlantic, first by the hundreds and then by the thousands. They couldn't all stay in Jamestown, for they had to clear the forests and plant the fields. There were no roads in Virginia, but the land was split by four great rivers coming down from the mountains to the Chesapeake Bay — the Potomac, the Rappahannock, the York, and the James. Each river had smaller rivers and creeks emptying into it; so it was easy for a boat to go from Jamestown far into the back country. The colonists soon formed a scheme for distributing the people. Explorers went up and down the rivers finding good places for set-tlements, where a few people could live close to-gether for company and safety, and yet have plenty of land nearby for the crops.

These places were called Hundreds, after the old English name for a division of a county. Perhaps in the beginning they were so called because there were a hundred people in each, but in Virginia the number was more likely to be a dozen or a score than a hundred. Each was a center for the farm lands about it and — which is the important thing — each was a little different from the others. Most of them were tobacco centers, but one was located at an iron mine, and another at a salt works on the seashore. Each had its own problems and none was exactly like Jamestown.

This meant that the job of running Virginia was no longer simple. John Smith, standing in the middle of Jamestown, could see almost the whole colony and he knew by name every white man in it. But a dozen years later the Hundreds spread up the James, up the York, and along the shores of Chesapeake Bay so far that it took days to travel to some of them. The governor no longer had everything under his own eyes and this led to more and more trouble.

The Company didn't help, either. This was not altogether the Company's fault, for life in Virginia was rough, and it was not easy to get good men for governors. They changed rapidly, and several were so unfit for the job that they nearly ruined the colony. One who made rather a mess of things was George Yeardley, who held the job in 1616 and part of 1617 and then returned to England. Two years later he was knighted and made governor again, and this time he seemed determined to make a go of it.

Perhaps his earlier failure had taught him something. Anyhow, in 1619 he was wise enough to know that he couldn't look after everything, or know what was best to be done in all the scattered Hundreds. So he sent out an order to each of the settlements to choose two good men and send them to Jamestown to help him make laws for the whole colony. They named the group the House of Burgesses. It was what we call a representative assembly, the first in America. Their rules and regulations were different, but the idea of choosing the Burgesses was exactly the idea by which we now choose members of the Congress of the United States.

These three ideas — first, that the man on the job knows best how to do it, or as we sometimes say, local management of local affairs; second, if you fail at one job try another, which is what is called economic mobility; and third, laws made by elected Burgesses, which is representative government — these three have been regarded as good ideas by Americans ever since. No other country has adopted them as completely as we have, so they may be called very American ideas.

Yet not one of them was adopted because some man sat down with pencil and paper, thought it all out, and wrote it down for other people to follow. All of them began because people got into some kind of jam and were trying to get out the best way they could. The London Company wanted wood and wood products; but the colonists took to cultivating the land, not because they hated the Company but because they had to eat. That was local management.

John Rolfe never said to himself, "I am going to be a tobacco planter because it is a grand and glorious thing to be a tobacco planter." He turned to that job because it was the best way of making a living. That was economic mobility.

Sir George Yeardley did not call the Burgesses because he had figured it out that it is the right of freeborn Englishmen to govern themselves, but because he needed their help in his complicated job. That was representative government.

All these things happened because America was America and not England. Later, on several occasions, men did sit down and figure out on paper beautiful schemes of government for various American colonies. The second Lord Baltimore made one for Maryland. William Penn made one for New Jersey and later for Pennsylvania. The philosopher John Locke made a very fancy one for the Carolinas. But none of them worked. Baltimore's and Penn's both had to be changed very largely, and the one made by the wisest man in England, Locke, was the one that failed most completely.

At the start nobody intended to become an American, but everybody did if he stayed in this country. They were changed simply by living in the new country. It was a great many years before many of them realized it. As late as 1775, more than a century and a half after Jamestown was founded, George Washington still thought of himself as a trueborn Englishman, although it was impossible for him to be anything of the sort.

What made us Americans was not long and careful thinking about it, but simply seeing what had to be done and doing it. What had to be done here was not exactly what had to be done in England; and in doing it we became something different from Englishmen.

CHAPTER FIVE

Freedom Gains — and Loses

TWO MEN very active in the Virginia Company were brothers, Edwin and George Sandys. They were sons of the Archbishop of York, which meant that they were much higher in English society than such men as John Smith and John Rolfe. Edwin, in fact, was a knight.

But they were more than merely highborn. Like Sir Walter Raleigh they had strong minds, interested in making money, but interested in a great many other things, too. George Sandys came to Virginia, studied the country, and wrote books about it. He was fond of writing verses, too, so he became the first American poet to write in English.

Sir Edwin Sandys stayed in England, where he became treasurer of the Company and what might be called its general manager. He was full of ideas, one of which was so unusual that people have never forgotten it. All the first settlers at Jamestown were men, and in the next four or five years nearly all the others who came were men, which meant that the colonists had no wives, except for a few, like John Rolfe, who married Indian women. To balance things Sir Edwin persuaded a number of young English girls to go to the colony, promising to try and find husbands for them there.

When the first group arrived, the colonists were told that any man who wanted a wife might marry one of the girls, provided she was willing and the colonist would pay her fare. But there was no money in Virginia except what had been brought in by the few ships that had come to Jamestown. There was no mint for making money, and not much gold and silver out of which to make it; so, since the colonists could not pay cash, the Company agreed to let them pay in tobacco, which the Company would take back to London and sell for cash. In those days the cost of carrying a person across the Atlantic was figured at something between five and ten pounds, English money, or, in our money, between twenty-five and fifty dollars. In London, at the time, tobacco sold for about a shilling a pound, so it was decided that a hundred and forty pounds of tobacco would be about right. One hundred and forty shillings were seven pounds sterling, or nearly thirty-five dollars.

This gave rise to the story that Sir Edwin Sandys sold wives for a hundred and forty pounds of tobacco each. That wasn't true. The girls were not sold, they did not have to marry, and if they did the tobacco was merely their passage money. But as it worked out all, or nearly all, married very promptly, so the scheme pleased everyone.

Sir Edwin Sandys had another idea that didn't work out exactly as he thought it would, but which was tremendously important for the United States. In England at this time the Christians had begun to hate each other more intensely than most of them hated the devil. It began with a row between Catholics and Protestants, but as soon as the Catholics lost out the Protestants began to quarrel among themselves. Elizabeth the Great had decreed that the Anglican Church, in this country now called the Episcopal Church, should represent the official religion. Some Protestants didn't like it. They said that the Anglican Church was nothing but a sort of watered-down Catholic Church, and would have none of it.

So the police, who were already making things hard for the Catholics, began making them hard for the Protestants who did not like the Church of England. To us, this seems a wicked thing to do, and so it was; but to most people at that time it didn't seem wicked. Many honest people thought that if a man did not believe in the king's religion he would not respect the king's authority; therefore all differences in religion must be put down, or there would be no law in the land.

One group of these Protestants found things getting too hard to be borne any longer. They were really good people; they had no wish to harm the king or to break the law, yet they felt that they had to do something. Their problem was solved when they found a verse in the Bible that reads: "Come out from among them and be ye separate, saith the Lord." II Corinthians, 6:17. So they called themselves Separatists, and decided to get out of England. They went to Holland, where the government cared very little what religion you professed as long as you obeyed the law.

But soon they were as unhappy there as they had been in England. The truth is that the Separatists were really exactly like their neighbors in the main thing: they believed that religion had to be a part of government and that if you had only one government you could have only one religion. So this group of English people were as horrified by the Dutch, who didn't care what they believed, as by the king of England, who did care and tried to make them believe what he believed.

Sir Edwin Sandys heard about them. He also heard that they were honest, hard-working people and, in everything except religion, peaceful and law-abiding. He thought they would make fine colonists, and in Virginia it would be easy to set them down a hundred or two hundred miles from their nearest white neighbors, so that they could follow any religion they liked without bothering anybody or being bothered.

He got in touch with their leaders and they soon came to an agreement. These people were different from most of the colonists sent to Jamestown in that they had money, so the contract made with them was different. They were not to be taken to Jamestown, but to some other part of Virginia. Once they were settled, the Company agreed to sell them land and allow them to pay for their transportation and supplies on easy terms; and as long as they kept up the payments the Company agreed not to interfere in their local affairs, especially their religion.

By this time the people had traveled about so much — from England to Holland, from Holland back to England, and now to America — that they dropped the name of Separatists and began to call themselves Pilgrims. The first group sailed on a ship called the *Speedwell*, which must have been a pretty bad one, because she sprung a leak before they were

well started and had to turn back. But they chartered another, called the *Mayflower,* and finally she made the crossing.

It was a long and terrible voyage, and before they came in sight of land, in November, 1620, the passengers were so utterly weary of the sea that they determined to land at the first place they could reach. The ship captains of those days were usually bad navigators, and the captain of the *Mayflower* was an unusually bad one. He not only missed Jamestown, he missed it by more than five hundred miles and didn't even touch the land belonging to the London Company. The Pilgrims landed far up in the territory assigned to the Plymouth Company; but they refused to do any more seafaring, and settled on the shores of a bay to which they gave the Indian name of Massachusetts.

It was all right. Sir Edwin Sandys willingly transferred the contract to the Plymouth Company, which became active at last. Once the Pilgrims had opened the way, a great many other Protestants, not dissatisfied enough to become Pilgrims but still dissatisfied, began to come to America. These were the Puritans, so called because they wanted to purify the Church of England. They settled across the bay from the Pilgrims' town of Plymouth, and founded Boston.

Eighteen years after Jamestown was founded and five years after the *Mayflower* sailed, King James died and his son Charles became king. Charles the First as king of England had to be a Protestant and publicly he pretended to like it, but privately he encouraged the Catholics as much as he dared, and everybody knew it. Perhaps he believed in the Catholic faith, but he wasn't very religious in anything else, so many people think he really cared nothing about any church but simply wanted to keep things stirred up, so that he could keep more power in his own hands.

If that was true, he succeeded too well for his own good. He kept things stirred up, all right. In the end he stirred up a civil war, which the Protestants won, and they promptly cut off the king's head. It served him right, for any king who leads his country into war when war could be avoided ought to lose his head.

But it took a long time — to be exact, twenty-four years — to bring on war. In the early days King Charles was pretty careful. He favored the Catholics, but usually in ways that nobody could object to very seriously. For instance, one of his favorite courtiers was a man named George Calvert, who had worked for King James as an ambassador and as one of the chief ministers of the Crown, but above all as a smart politician; and just before King James's death Calvert, who had been a Protestant like all his family, suddenly turned Catholic. It meant that he had to resign his seat in Parliament and his political offices; but the new king kept him as a member of the Privy Council, which was a group of advisers to the king chosen by the king himself, not by Parliament. King Charles made Calvert an Irish baron, since he owned an estate in Ireland as well as one in England. In those days a baron usually took his title from the name of his estate, so Calvert took the Irish title of Lord Baltimore.

But although the Baron of Baltimore had quit politics, he remained a very smart man. He could still see what was coming better than most of the people around him. Things were already bad for Catholics in England, and Baltimore could see that they were likely to grow worse, rather than better; so he, like the Pilgrims, began to think of America as a place where his people could practice their religion without bothering or being bothered by anybody else.

Besides that, he knew, as the Pilgrims and Puritans knew, and everybody else knew, that America was a very rich continent in which fortunes could be made by men who would work hard with their hands, and think as well as John Rolfe thought when

150

he discovered how to cure tobacco. The Pilgrims, the Puritans, and the Catholics all wanted first to escape religious persecution; but they wanted to make money, too, and they believed that moving to America would serve both purposes.

The Pilgrims and the Puritans were Protestants, so their case was much simpler. If the London Company and the Plymouth Company chose to give them land, the other Protestants didn't care. Besides, the two Companies were private corporations and the government was not directly responsible for what they did. But by 1624 the London Company had gone bankrupt and the Plymouth Company had simply faded away; the Crown had taken over all English claims in America and people who wished to go there dealt directly with the king.

So when Baltimore made his proposal to settle Catholics in America, King Charles had something to worry about. He was willing, but what would the Protestant Parliament say about royal favors to Catholics? Baltimore, the smooth politician, had an answer. Somewhere he had discovered a document more than eight hundred years old, by which an English king had set up in England what was called the Palatinate of Durham. A palatinate is a sort of state within a state—an area over which the king gives most of his authority to an officer called a palatine. In Durham, England, the Bishop of Durham was the palatine.

Baltimore copied this document almost word for word, except that where it said "bishop" he substituted "Baron of Baltimore," and where it said "Durham" he substituted "Maryland." This was a smart touch, for the queen's first name was Maria, or in its English form, Mary, and Baltimore knew that the queen would be pleased at having the country named for her.

But the smartest touch of all was the one new clause that Baltimore wrote into the old Durham charter. It was a stern order that the new palatine must under no circumstances interfere with the Protestant religion. Take note that he said "Protestant" only. Since he, Baltimore, was to be the palatine, and since he was a Catholic himself, there was no fear that he would interfere with the Catholic religion, and he could safely leave it out.

So when the king laid the charter before his Protestant officials he could say truthfully that the only mention of religion in the document was a clause making Protestants safe. They couldn't object to that. Of course they figured it for a trick and they growled and grumbled, but there really wasn't much they could do about it without looking ridiculous, so in the end they let it go through.

However, it was two years before everything was straightened out, and before the Great Seal had actually been applied to make the charter official George Calvert had died; so it was issued to his son, Cecilius, the second Lord Baltimore.

He lost no time. By 1634, fourteen years after Massachusetts, and twenty-seven years after Virginia, Maryland was founded as the third English colony. The important thing about it was that, in order to get the charter at all, George Calvert had had to fix things so that in Maryland nobody could be persecuted for his religion. This idea worked. In fact, it worked so well that it was adopted in other charters and gradually spread through the other colonies. By the time the Revolution was won it was so firmly fixed in the American mind that it was written into the Constitution of the United States. That is how freedom of religion became one of the basic principles of our government.

When war at last broke out between King Charles the First and Parliament, Parliament's navy was commanded, and very ably, too, by Admiral Sir William Penn. But the heavy fighting was on land, where the very rough but very great soldier, Oliver Cromwell, first beat the king, and after the king was beheaded, beat Parliament, becoming dictator of

England, although he gave himself the title of Lord Protector.

Cromwell ruled England well and the country grew richer and greater under him, but it cannot be denied that he was harsh, and the English have never liked dictators anyhow. Soon Cromwell and his party, which consisted mostly of Puritans who had not gone to America, came to be hated as bitterly as King Charles had been, but nobody was tough enough to stand up against Cromwell. After eleven years, however, he died and there was nobody his equal to take his place. So General Monk, who now commanded the army, and Admiral Penn got in touch with the exiled son of the former king and brought him back to England as King Charles II. This made Penn a favorite of the new king, even though he had served Parliament for a while.

But the hard-fighting old admiral had a son who was the great worry of his life. It was not that the boy, who was named after his father, was stupid or wicked; on the contrary, he was rather too good for his father's taste. Sir William was not a bad man, but he was a tough sailor who had spent the best years of his life at sea and he knew much more about battles and storms than he did about Bibles and churches. So when his son William became extremely interested in religion, the old admiral feared that there was something sickly about it and he did everything he could to turn the boy's thoughts in some other direction. William was a dutiful son and for a long time he did whatever his father told him to. He went to sea for a while, and when a rebellion broke out in Ireland he joined the army and fought well enough to win praise from his superior officers. He was sent on some important errands for the king and did them well, too, for he had a fine mind.

Yet he did not really want to be an admiral, a general, or an ambassador. For a while he studied law and his mind was brilliant enough to master it in a short time; he could have done well in the law, but he didn't want to be a judge, or even chancellor of England. He thought constantly of religion; but it was religion itself he was thinking of, not the church. He didn't want to be a bishop. As he grew older he decided that real religion was not fairly represented by any of the four principal churches — the Anglican, the Catholic, the Presbyterian, or the Independent, which later became known as the Congregational. He decided that he found more real religion in what was then a small sect, despised by all the churches and treated as heretics by the police.

These people had two main ideas. One was that all worldly pomp and show is vanity, usually sinful and always foolish. The other was that for men to kill each other even in battle is murder, directly against the law of God. They did not call themselves a church, only a society; and because of their hatred of quarreling that leads to war they named their group the Society of Friends. Their enemies, trying to make the world believe that they refused to fight because they were afraid, scornfully called them Quakers.

This group young Penn joined, much to the distress of old Sir William. In a way Penn repeated the story of George Calvert, who also gave up a great career to join a persecuted sect. One joined the Catholics and the other the Quakers, but for the same reason. Both thought religion more important than any worldly honors.

One thing we ought to remember to the honor of the old admiral. He never understood his son, and when the police popped William into jail for writing a pamphlet that the bishops didn't like, his father was dreadfully embarrassed. Yet, although he was an admiral, accustomed to giving orders and having them obeyed, he never tried to drive the boy, and when he died William was at his bedside and they were the best of friends.

King Charles the Second was always careless about money matters, and as a result was nearly always hard up. Sir William Penn was one of many who lent him money and never got it back; most of them never got anything back, but Sir William's son was a lawyer, and when he inherited the debt he saw a way to get something for it, even if he couldn't recover the cash. He offered to settle the account if the king would give him land in America, and Charles was glad to do it that way. Like the Protestant Pilgrims and the Catholic Baltimore, Penn had decided that his people would do well to get out of England to a place where they could practice their religion undisturbed.

The king fell in with the plan. The map showed

that Virginia had been granted the land along the coast up to the thirty-eighth parallel and inland to the south bank of the Potomac River, while Baltimore had been granted the land from the thirty-eighth to the fortieth parallel; so Penn was granted two degrees north of Baltimore's land, that is, from forty to forty-two, a little less than a hundred and forty miles from south to north. Westward from the coast it had no limit, except what was vaguely known as the "South Sea" and nobody knew exactly where that was.

On the coast this took in what is now known as New Jersey, and Penn sent his first colony there. But some other settlers had already drifted in from various places and disputes arose about the real ownership of the land. True to his religious dislike of quarreling, Penn chose to give up New Jersey and move his colony across the Delaware River, since there was no doubt whatever about his title to the west bank. At that time it was all thickly wooded, so he took *sylva*, the Latin word for "forest," and added it to his own name, calling the country Pennsylvania, or *Penn's woods*.

William Penn was a great lover of the classics. Not content with giving a half-Latin name to the colony, he gave a wholly Greek name to the town he established on a point of land where the Schuylkill River joins the Delaware. He had in mind the Quaker doctrine of living in peace when he named the town by a Greek word meaning the love of brothers, or Philadelphia.

As it happened, he was guilty of a decidedly unloving thing in this connection, for he built his town on Baltimore's land. He did not do so intentionally. He had his surveyors lay out what they thought was the fortieth parallel and built the town north of it; but surveyors' instruments were not very accurate in those days, and most surveyors didn't know their job any too well. These men put the line several miles too far south; the real fortieth parallel runs through the middle of the modern city of Philadelphia. Later the Lords Baltimore sued to recover the land, but after a long argument it was decided that Penn had acted in good faith, and as he had already built his town he should be allowed to have it.

Nearly a hundred years later the two colonies employed Charles Mason and Jeremiah Dixon, two surveyors who really did know their business, to draw the line correctly. They fixed it at 39 degrees and 43 minutes, which left Philadelphia well up in Pennsylvania. A hundred years after that, the Mason and Dixon Line became famous as the boundary between the free and the slave states; and nearly a hundred years after the slaves were freed it is still famous as the line between the North and the South in the United States.

It was in 1684 that Penn established his colony, following the example of George Calvert by making religious freedom one of its principles. The difference is that Calvert had to do it in order to get his charter, while Penn would probably have done it anyhow, since tolerance is a Quaker principle.

The fifty years that had passed since the establishment of Maryland had brought a great many changes to England. There had been a revolution followed by eleven years without a king, and then a counterrevolution that brought the king back. All this fighting and arguing and dickering and dealing had convinced most Englishmen that to fight wars over religion was silly. Four years after the settlement of Philadelphia the English got rid of another king, but this time they did not consider it necessary to cut off his head. They merely sent him packing and put on the throne another, more to their liking.

Since even in England the idea of religious freedom was taking hold by 1684, the fact that William Penn believed in it did not startle people nearly as much as Baltimore had startled them fifty years earlier. The really new idea in Pennsylvania was not tolerance of different forms of Christianity; it was tolerance of out-and-out heathen. Penn thought that while the king of England had a right to be a king of America too, still the actual owners of the land were the Indians, and he did not think it right to take it from them by force. So he bought his land and paid for it. Before he allowed a single white man to settle in Pennsylvania he met with the Indian chiefs and they agreed to sell him a certain amount of land. As long as he lived Penn would not allow any white man to take one foot of land beyond the line that he and the chiefs had agreed on. The result was that he never had an Indian war.

Virginia, Massachusetts, Maryland, and Pennsylvania, in that order, were the four colonies that the English set up in a distinctly English way. In the end there were nine others, but eight of them were established in ways that were not especially English, or by repeating what had been done in the first four. The two Carolinas, for example, were a sort of repetition of what had been done in Virginia. Instead of a company, however, Charles the Second granted the land to eight of his favorites, who called themselves the Lords Proprietors. Since the Latin for Charles is Carolus, they called the whole area Carolina, in honor of the king, and employed the philosopher, John Locke, to draw up a model system of government for it.

They established Charleston in 1670 as the capital of the region, but later divided it into North and South Carolina, with the North Carolina capital at New Bern. Locke's scheme of government never worked, and what with one kind of trouble after another, seven of the Lords Proprietors were glad to sell out to the king in 1719. The other, Lord Granville, insisted on keeping his eighth, so they laid out one degree of latitude south of the Virginia border, and Granville and his heirs held it until 1776.

In fact, Granville held only a few miles back from the Atlantic Coast, but in theory it stretched to the Pacific Ocean, which made it, in theory, the biggest estate that one man ever held in America — nearly

70 miles wide and nearly 3000 miles long. But except for this odd circumstance the settlement of the Carolinas was much like that of Virginia.

New York was first settled by the Dutch, who, like William Penn, bought land from the Indians — the island of Manhattan, which they called New Amsterdam, and for which they paid the equivalent of twenty-four dollars in our money. Later, when war broke out between England and Holland, the British Navy seized New Amsterdam. The first time they gave it back, and the Dutch changed the name of the town to New Orange. When a second war came and the English seized it a second time they kept it, and changed the name to New York, in honor of the king's brother, the Duke of York.

But this method of getting a colony was not especially new and not especially English. All countries had been seizing the land of others in time of war since history began. Delaware was taken in the same way from the Swedes, who had settled near what is now New Castle, and who seem to have built the first log cabins in America. They had long known how to build with logs in Sweden, but neither the English nor the Dutch knew anything about it until the Swedes taught them.

The rest of New England was settled mostly by the gradual spreading out of people from Massachusetts. The process was speeded up by the Puritans, who, once they got a firm foothold in the new country, began to persecute other religions as vigorously as they had themselves been persecuted in England. Roger Williams, for instance, who had been a Puritan, turned into a Baptist and was promptly thrown out of Massachusetts with his followers. They settled Rhode Island. Others went of their own accord into Connecticut and New Hampshire.

But this, again, was not new and not English. All colonies of all nations tend to spread out, as they grow, and New England was no exception to the rule.

One other colony, however, began in a curious fashion. This was the one farthest south, Georgia, the thirteenth and the last of those that became the United States. It was founded by a soldier and a good man, but not good in the sense of being an enthusiastic churchman. General James Edward Oglethorpe belonged to the Church of England himself, but he was willing to let other people worship in whatever way seemed right to them, provided they lived what he regarded as the right kind of lives.

One hundred and twenty-five years after Jamestown was founded, this man and a group of his friends obtained a charter to found a colony south of South Carolina. There were three parties inter-

ested in this adventure — the government, Oglethorpe, and Oglethorpe's associates. They did not all
have the same things in mind. The government
thought of a buffer state to protect South Carolina
against the Spaniards in Florida and the French and
Indians to the west and southwest. The associates
thought of establishing a flourishing colony that
would bring in trade and make their land more
valuable. Oglethorpe thought of holding off the
Spaniards, as the government did, and of making
money as his associates did, but most of all of establishing a model government, free from the evils he
saw around him in England.

It is hard to understand General Oglethorpe. He
was a soldier and a good one, as he had proved in
many campaigns on the continent of Europe. He
knew how to lead soldiers, so he must have known
what soldiers are like. He knew that life in the new
colony would be rough and dangerous for some
years, so he needed first-rate fighting men as colonists. Yet in 1732 he set up rules as rigid as those the
Puritans had set up for Massachusetts in 1620, and
far more rigid than those Jamestown had set up in
1607. The Georgians could not drink, they could not
gamble, they could not hold slaves, they could not
oppress the Indians — all good rules, certainly, but
not the kind that many fighting men have ever kept.

Oglethorpe got the fighting men. He brought in former soldiers from England and from the continent of Europe, and he also brought in a large group of Scottish Highlanders, who have always been good soldiers. They held off the Spaniards all right, and at one time came near driving them out of northern Florida. They held off the Indians and the French. They kept South Carolina safe from invasion. But they hated Oglethorpe's rules and broke them constantly. They drank and they gambled and they bought slaves and they cheated the Indians at every opportunity. In the end Oglethorpe gave up the project and decided to turn the colony over to the king.

Yet there was something very English about General James Oglethorpe. No other country has produced so many fine generals who were also intensely pious men. Oliver Cromwell and "Chinese" Gordon (His real name was Charles, but they called him Chinese on account of his campaigns in China) were generals very much like Oglethorpe, and America produced one in Thomas Jonathan (called "Stonewall") Jackson.

So it may be said that Oglethorpe brought to America something that neither John Smith nor the Puritans nor George Calvert nor William Penn had. Maybe they had a little of it, but not nearly as much as Oglethorpe. This was the idea that government, without interfering with religion, can make men better by wise laws and regulations. It is true that Oglethorpe's laws were not always wise, and it is doubtful that they made the early Georgians any better, but the idea was there and it remained after Oglethorpe had gone back to England. In fact, it remains a part of American tradition to this day.

These were the thirteen colonies that became the United States: Massachusetts, New Hampshire, Rhode Island, Connecticut, New York, New Jersey, Pennsylvania, Delaware, Maryland, Virginia, North Carolina, South Carolina, and Georgia. When Georgia was founded, Quebec was still French, but both France and England claimed Nova Scotia and Newfoundland as colonies. Some effort was made to persuade them to go along with the others in 1776, but nothing came of it.

In the hundred years after 1607 many people came to America from other places than the British Isles, and some of them made an impression on the country that can still be seen. The Swedes did not hold Delaware long enough to leave many traces, but in New York there are still numerous families with Dutch names — the Roosevelts are the most famous but the Van Burens gave us one president —

and France held Louisiana so long that many people in that state still speak a kind of French.

However, the English did not mind having people of other nations move into their colonies if they were peaceable, hard-working folk. For instance, Baron de Graffenried in 1710 brought a large colony of Swiss into North Carolina, and a little later Count Zinzendorf, a German, brought Moravians into Pennsylvania. Oglethorpe brought other Moravians into Georgia, although when fighting broke out along the border most of them, being pacifists, moved to Salem, in North Carolina. Many other Germans of persecuted sects moved into Pennsylvania and spread to other colonies. By 1700 there were Jews from Spain and Portugal in every town of any size, but they did not settle in groups, as the Swiss did in New Bern, North Carolina, and the Moravians in Bethlehem, Pennsylvania, to make a small part of America not English at all.

But of all the non-British people who came in the early days, the ones who had the most conspicuous and most lasting effect on the country did not come here of their own free will. In 1619, a full year before the *Mayflower* sailed from England, a Dutch ship came into Jamestown and sold the colonists commodities of various kinds, among them being what a writer at the time described as "twenty negurs."

He meant Negroes, slaves brought from the West African coast, and sold to the colonists as if they had been so many cows or horses. Nobody saw anything wrong with this at the time, but it was a great crime, and later America paid for it with a fearful civil war and with many kinds of troubles, some of which have lasted to this day.

It is interesting to note that the first elected law-makers, the Virginia House of Burgesses, out of which our Congress grew, met for the first time in 1619; and in that same year the first Negro slaves

were brought into the country. So a full year before the Pilgrims landed in Massachusetts, two ideas that could not possibly exist together in the same country forever — freedom and slavery — had been planted in America. One of these ideas had to go; and if freedom finally won, it was only after centuries of bitter struggle, during which deeds of heroism and horrible crimes were frequent on both sides. The plain right and wrong of it became so confused that for many years the best men in the country didn't know what they ought to do.

CHAPTER SIX

English Is Spoken Here

IN THE course of time English-speaking people took over all the land that is now the United States, and because of that we who live in it today often forget that any other people had much to do with the discovery and settlement of the country.

The truth is, though, that for two hundred years it was doubtful whether America would finally become an English- or a Spanish- or a French-speaking country. As we have seen, when Columbus sailed and for a hundred years afterward Spain and France were the only two countries in Europe that were really great powers. Portugal and Holland were both regarded as more important than England. Germany and Italy didn't exist; the land they now occupy was cut up into a great number of small nations, some calling themselves kingdoms, some duchies, some principalities, and some republics. Far to the east was a land the rest of Europe knew almost nothing about. It was called Muscovy and its ruler was a Grand Duke. About the time Columbus sailed, this Grand Duke, Ivan III, overthrew the Tartars, a Mongolian people who had held part of the land for centuries, and thereafter he gave himself a new title. He would no longer be a grand duke, he would be the "Caesar" of Muscovy, or, as they spelled it in Moscow, the czar. That was the beginning of Russia, but centuries passed before she became a great power.

From 1492 to 1763, more than two hundred and fifty years, the fate of America depended on what happened in Europe. At the start, France and Spain seemed to have everything their own way, but little by little England grew stronger. She broke the sea power of Spain by defeating the Invincible Armada in 1588. A hundred and seventy-one years later she broke the sea power of France at the battle of Quiberon Bay in 1759. Both France and Spain remained strong on land, but no European nation except a great sea power could hold America, and by 1763 England was the greatest sea power of them all. So from that time on America was definitely English.

Still, before they lost control by losing wars at sea, both the Spanish and the French did many wonderful things in America, and many of the most romantic tales in our history are told about their explorers.

173

For instance, there was the Spanish Governor of Cuba, Ponce de León. He had reached the age of fifty-three and felt that he was getting old, when some liar came to him in 1513 with the tale that in the island of Bimini, somewhere to the north, there was a wonderful fountain whose water, drunk by an old man, would make him young again. De León at once set out to find the Fountain of Youth. He never discovered Bimini, which perhaps was just as well, for it meant that he never discovered how foolish he had been to think that there was such a thing as the Fountain of Youth. But he did discover a large body of land that nobody had seen before. He sighted it on Easter Sunday, which in Spain was called the Feast of Flowers (in Spanish *Pascua Florida*), so he named the land Florida, which it has been called ever since.

A few years later there came Hernando (we would call him Ferdinand) de Soto. He landed in Florida and pushed northward as far as what is now North Carolina, then crossed the mountains — probably the first white man to do so — and moved west. After many days' traveling he came to the Mississippi. No white man had ever seen it before.

De Soto crossed it and went a little way into what is now Arkansas. But he had been having trouble with the Indians all the way. He kept losing men, some killed by the Indians, some dying of disease and hardship. He had lost nearly all his horses, some killed, some stolen by Indians. Some people think that De Soto's horses were the first brought into the United States, and that the ones the Indians stole were taken west and became the ancestors of the Indian ponies found in the West a hundred years later. At last De Soto gave up and turned back to the river.

But then he himself caught some kind of disease, probably a malarial fever, and died in a few days. His men, the few that were left, faced a problem. De Soto was a fine soldier, and the Indians were more afraid of him than of any other white man, and they hated him as much as they feared him. If they discovered that he was dead, they would gloat; and if the white men buried the body the Indians would certainly dig it up, and in their savage way would make a mockery of it. So De Soto's men built rafts and got on them with the body one dark night. Then when they were well out from the bank, they weighted the body and sank it in the middle of the river, so that no man has ever known where the bones of De Soto lie. The rest of the men floated down the river to its mouth and so made their way back to the Spanish colonies.

But the most remarkable of all tales of the Spanish

explorations is one that might be called "The Long Walk of Stephen the Slave." This man may have had another name, but all we know is that the Spaniards called him Esteban, the Spanish for Stephen. He was a black man, perhaps a Moor, perhaps a Negro. He was taken along by a Spanish commander named Narváez, who landed at what is now Tampa, Florida, with four hundred people to found a colony. But Narváez wasn't really interested in colonies. All he had on his mind was gold, so instead of settling down to cultivate the land, he marched up the length of Florida and then turned west to about where the city of Tallahassee is now.

By that time, he had decided, quite rightly, that there wasn't any gold in that part of the country, so he built boats and tried to get back to Mexico, where he had come from. He never made it. He did get past the mouth of the Mississippi, but a storm caught him off the coast of Texas, wrecked the boats, and drowned Narváez and most of his people. The few who did manage to get ashore were picked off by the Indians, until at last there were only two left, Esteban and a Spaniard named Cabeza de Vaca, and they were captives. The Indians carried them north and west, passing them along from tribe to tribe. Years passed. Cabeza de Vaca and Esteban learned the languages of various tribes, learned the customs of the Indians, learned how to hunt and fish and trap like Indians, almost became Indians themselves. Finally, the Indians became friendly enough to let them go south, and in 1536, eight years after the shipwreck, they turned up in Mexico City. If you measure on a map from somewhere near Beaumont, Texas, up into New Mexico and then down to Mexico City, you will see that Esteban's stroll, up to this point, had been about two thousand miles; but he had just started walking.

Among other things the two men learned from the Indians was any number of tall tales. Some were about the Indian gods and what made the thunder and lightning, and all that sort of thing, but they

didn't seem to pay much attention to that. They didn't believe any of it, because they didn't want to believe it. They were both good Christians. But when the Indians talked of the wonderful land of Cibola, to the northwest, and of its seven cities built mostly of gold, Esteban and Cabeza de Vaca wanted to believe and they did believe.

Historians today think that what the Indians had in mind were the seven pueblos of the Zuñis in northwest New Mexico. These pueblos, as a matter of fact, were rather wonderful as compared to the settlements of other Indians, but they were a long way from being built of gold. Some of them were built of stone and others of adobe, that is to say, bricks made of sun-dried mud; and what little gold was in them was in the form of ornaments and trinkets of various kinds. The Zuñi people had learned how to build houses and cultivate the land, which put them ahead of other Indians, but they were not wealthy as the Spaniards counted wealth.

However, when the two survivors of Narváez's expedition got to Mexico City, Cabeza de Vaca not only talked incessantly but also wrote long stories about the seven cities of Cibola, and soon all the Spaniards in Mexico were wild to find them. This was not as foolish as it seems to us today. After all, the city of Mexico, when Cortes found it, had contained enormous treasure, and the city of Cuzco, in Peru, when Pizarro found it, had contained even more. Why, then, shouldn't there be a Cibola, richer than either?

But it was not for Cabeza de Vaca. He had had enough. Eight years of wandering in that tremendous country had made him willing to leave the seven cities of Cibola to anyone who could find them; as for him, he went home to Spain.

That left Esteban as the only man who knew the country. So he started walking again, perhaps willingly, perhaps because he had no choice. His leader this time was Marcos de Niza, a Franciscan missionary usually known as Fray (that is, Brother) Marcos. After a march of some eight hundred miles, much of it through desert country and very tough going indeed, they actually reached a Zuñi pueblo, somewhere in New Mexico or Arizona.

This was the end of the road for Stephen. Fray Marcos had a few white men and some Indian guides with him, and he feared the Zuñis would think they were a war party; so Stephen, who spoke many Indian languages, was sent ahead to say that the visitors meant no harm. He seems to have been able to talk to the people in the pueblo and they let him in, but after he had told his story there was a long debate. Some said these people must be the white gods about whom Indians who had been to Mexico had been telling stories. But others said that was nonsense; real gods would not send a black man as their messenger, so this fellow must be a fraud trying to trap the Zuñis into some dangerous scheme. Most of the pueblo people decided that this view was the true one, so they killed poor Stephen and threw his body outside.

That was enough for Fray Marcos. He went away from there as fast as he could and returned to Mexico. After all that traveling perhaps his legs were pretty well worn-out anyhow. But his imagination was still lively. He hadn't found anything except a new kind of Indian house, but he swallowed all the tales that were told him and even seems to have added a touch of his own. Not only were the cities of Cibola filled with gold, the doors of the houses were studded with turquoise.

Of course this called for a more thorough exploration, which was entrusted to Francisco Vasquez de Coronado, Governor of Nueva Galicia, the northwest part of Spanish Mexico. Coronado reached the pueblos all right, and when he found what they were Fray Marcos very nearly lost his head, and he did lose his reputation.

The Indians, however, were still full of tales. Probably their intention was to get rid of a lot of troublesome visitors by sending them on to the next tribe. At any rate, they persuaded Coronado that the richest of all the cities of Cibola was one called Quivira, which seemed always to be just a few miles farther on. Coronado split up his command into several detachments. One discovered Lower California, one the Grand Canyon of the Colorado, one the Panhandle country of Texas, and one eastern Kansas; but Quivira was not found. Coronado considered himself a failure, but as a matter of fact he had explored more of the United States than any other one man, and is still remembered for that reason.

The three great nations came into America from three directions: the Spanish from the south, the French from the north, the English from the east. Thus the Spanish got the hot part of the continent, the French got the cold part, and the English got the temperate in-between part. The Spanish came first, a few directly from Spain, but more by way of Cuba and Mexico. The English and French came directly from England and France, the French just barely in advance of the English. A Frenchman named Jacques Cartier tried and failed to settle Canada forty years before Sir Walter Raleigh tried and failed in North Carolina; and one named Pierre du Guast, better known as the Sieur (which meant Lord) de Monts did settle Nova Scotia in 1603, four years before the English landed at Jamestown.

The French were especially interested in the great river which they named after Saint Lawrence. They thought it would lead them right through America to what they called the South Sea and we now call the Pacific Ocean. Like other Europeans, they had no idea of the enormous size of North America, and they were astonished when they pushed up the river to find that it led, not to any salt sea, but to a series of immense fresh-water lakes. Even when they had reached the western end of the Great Lakes they did not dream that they were still on the eastern side of the continent.

The settlement that De Monts made on Nova Scotia has a romantic interest for citizens of the United States, not that it was very important in itself but because an American writer made it important. The Micmac Indians, who roamed over the country when the French arrived, called it Akade, which meant something like "place of plenty." The French made it Acadie, and the English, Acadia. The land, lying near the sea, had a more temperate climate than most of Canada, and farm crops flourished, especially in the region called Grand Pré, or in English, Great Meadow. So the colony prospered for more than a hundred years.

In 1621, seventeen years after the French colony was established, James 1 of England renamed the country Nova Scotia, Latin for "New Scotland," and gave it to one of his subjects, Sir William Alexander. It wasn't his to give, but a little thing like that never bothered King James; he was stingy enough with his own possessions, but generous with other people's property, so he had no hesitation in giving a French colony to an English knight. To do him justice, the king thought pretty much like everybody else in Europe at the time. Most people believed quite sincerely that land in America belonged to anyone who could take it and keep it.

Unfortunately, Sir William was not equal to the task. He sent out a colony and it reached the new country; but there were too many French people already there. The English were not exactly thrown out. After all, settlers were needed and apparently the French preferred an Englishman to nobody, so the newcomers were just swallowed up and after a few years became French in all but name.

However, James's gift to Sir William was remembered, and long years afterward it gave the English an excuse for claiming the land. When a hundred and fifty years had passed, and England had grown strong enough to have a chance against France, a series of great wars broke out. Then this Acadia, or

Nova Scotia, became important, because, lying at the mouth of the St. Lawrence, it was a key position. It was fought over time after time, captured and re-captured. By that time there were about ten thousand people in the Grand Pré region, and they were supplying the French with a great many first-class fighting men.

So the English did a very cruel and unjust thing. They put the Acadians on ships and scattered them among the British colonies from Maine to Georgia. The worst of it was that they did not have ships enough to move them all together, so they sent the men first, and the women and children followed

later. The result was that many families were broken up; women never again saw their husbands, or children their fathers.

This affair touches the history of the United States in two ways. Some of these people made their way to Louisiana, then still French, and settled there. To this day a part of the state of Louisiana is inhabited by people who call themselves Acadians (which has been corrupted into Cajuns) and speak a kind of French. That was the first way in which they became part of our history. The second was that their story was written many years later by the American poet Longfellow, in a long poem called *Evangeline*, which was so much admired that parts of it were

taught to every American school child for a hundred years. It is not much read now, although it is a pretty good poem if you like sadly sentimental verse.

For many years it seemed likely that the continent of North America would be like the continent of Europe, divided into many nations speaking different languages. Even that part which is now the United States was split up. People spoke Dutch in New York; Swedish in New Castle, Delaware; Spanish in Florida; French in Louisiana; English elsewhere — not counting the Indians, who spoke languages of their own, which had never been heard in Europe.

But it didn't work out that way. In the end, the whole country spoke English as the official language except in the one state of New Mexico, where Spanish and English are both official.

The official language is the one in which the laws of a country are written. An American in his own house can speak and write any language he chooses. Nobody cares. But when he applies for a birth certificate to prove who he is, or a license to marry, or when he gets a deed to a house and lot, or any other legal document, it is written in English. When a case is tried in court, everyone concerned must either speak English himself or get an interpreter to speak it for him. In the courts of New Mexico one may speak either English or Spanish, but no other language.

To understand how English came to be the official language in almost the whole of this country, one must drop the history of the United States for a moment and look at what was happening in Europe.

For years the settlers on this continent regarded themselves as belonging to the country from which they came. There were Englishmen in Massachusetts and Virginia, Frenchmen in Louisiana, Spaniards in Florida, and so on. There was no such thing as an American, unless you count the Indians as Americans. No one who came, or whose people came from Europe — and this included all the white people — called himself an American.

This was a mistake, as we shall see when we get further along in the story. These people were really quite different from what their fathers had been, or what they themselves had been when they lived in Europe. But they didn't know it. It was a long, long time before they realized that simply living in a new country, with a different climate and different soil and different plants and animals, makes a man think and act differently from the way he thought and acted in the old country.

All this, though, was discovered later. About the

year 1707, when Jamestown was a hundred years
old, white people living in America still thought of
themselves as English or French or whatever they
had been before they came here. So no matter what
happened to England, the people in Virginia felt
that they had to go along; no matter what happened
to Spain, the people in Florida went along; and so
with all the others. This is why the fate of America
was settled, not by what happened here, but by
what happened in Europe.

We have noticed that when the French settled
Nova Scotia, in 1604, and the English settled Virginia, in 1607, the two great powers in Europe were
Spain and France, with England coming up fast,
but not yet a really great power. During the next
hundred years Spain was going down and England
was coming up, with France pretty much holding
her own.

There were many reasons for this. In fact, there
were so many that large numbers of learned men
have spent their lives trying to figure them all out,
and are still disputing over which was the most important. Back in the old days it used to be thought
that the English were simply better fighters than
anybody else, but you can't prove it. Neither England nor France ever had better fighters than the
five hundred Spaniards who went with Cortes to

Mexico. The English were beaten in many battles during these years, yet England steadily came up and Spain as steadily went down.

As far as fighting is concerned, the main difference seems to be that the English fought best on the sea, while both Spain and France were at their best on land. In the seventeenth century (1601-1700) an English army was often second-rate, an English fleet almost never. Since the sea was the road to America, this gave the English an enormous advantage in holding colonies.

But there was more to it than that. The Spanish, too, were good sea fighters — not quite as good as the English, perhaps, but good enough to hold Mexico and South America. It was not any lack of bravery or skill in her fighting men that caused Spain slowly to go down.

Bad government had more to do with it than poor fighting, and one of the worst faults of the Spanish kings was that they never understood much about wealth. Because they were getting enormous quantities of gold (and in later years chocolate, sugar, and tobacco worth more than the gold) from America they considered themselves rich. What they never could understand is that money is no good in itself; it is what you buy with it that counts.

The Spanish kings spent most of their money paying soldiers and buying weapons and gunpowder. They fought war after war, either to seize land that belonged to some other king, or to hold on to what they already had. Philip the Second spent an immense sum on the Invincible Armada to conquer England, although he really didn't need England. He lost it all and lost more than money — the English were never afraid of him again. In the Netherlands, on the seas, and in Italy the kings of Spain squandered their money, getting nothing for it in the end; and Spain sank gradually lower and lower.

By 1750 Spain was a second-rate power, and France and England were the big ones. England became still more powerful in 1707 when Scotland and England were united into the one kingdom of Great Britain. That name comes from the Romans, who, centuries earlier, had held all that part of the world. They called England Britannia Major and the nearby peninsula of Brittany in France Britannia Minor — in English, Great Britain and Little Britain.

As early as 1740 it was plain that a showdown was coming between Great Britain and France, and the colonies of each would be involved. From that time on there was war after war. Great Britain did not do any too well in Europe, but on the sea and in the colonies she began to get the upper hand, and the French were expelled from one part of the world after another. At that time the big prize was not America but India, and the struggle came to a climax in 1765 when, after seven years' fighting, the British drove the French out of both India and North America, except for Louisiana, and gained nearly complete mastery of the seas.

In all this fighting Spain usually sided with France, and so lost everything she had in eastern America except Florida — then called the Floridas because it was divided into East Florida (the present state) and West Florida (a strip along the Gulf of Mexico to Louisiana).

The people in America had very little to say about all this fighting. Whether British or French, they were dragged along whenever the mother countries fell out. But it was hard on them, because both British and French did everything they could to persuade the Indians to help and the Indians usually did, some of them joining the British, others the French.

But the Indians were still savages and their method of fighting was barbarous. In civilized Europe soldiers fought soldiers, but the Indians fought everybody. They killed women and children, as well as men, and when they took prisoners they frequently put them to death by cruel tortures. When they killed an enemy, they had a dreadful habit of

191

making a circular cut on the top of his head and then taking hold of the hair and pulling off the scalp, which they carried away as a trophy.

Naturally, the white people got a very bad opinion of the Indians. It wasn't entirely fair, because among the whites there were many bad characters, and when a fight broke out it was often a white man who started it. But angry men seldom stop to think of their own evil deeds, and when settlers came upon a place where a house had been burned and the owner, his wife, and his children horribly butchered by the Indians, they didn't ask who started it. They simply got their guns and went after those Indians. In the course of time they began to fight as savagely as the Indians themselves. In many cases the government itself forgot what it was to be civilized and offered a bounty — that is a money prize — for Indian scalps.

The war that ended in 1763 was called the French and Indian War by the Americans, but if you should mention it by that name to an English schoolboy he would not know what you were talking about. In his history books it is called the Seven Years' War.

The French and Indian War did two very important things. In the first place, it finished the Indians as a real threat to the white men. There were many Indian wars after 1763, but never again was there real danger that the Indians would sweep the whites out of the country. In the second place, the defeat of the French meant that this would be an English-speaking country. Up to that time it was a real question whether most Americans would speak English or French; but after 1763 it was English without a doubt, except in a few spots such as the lower part of Louisiana, where people still speak French, and New Mexico, where some still speak Spanish.

So it was in 1763 that the real history of what we know as the United States began.

CHAPTER SEVEN

The Colonies Fight

AS WE have seen, hardly anybody living on this continent in 1763 thought of himself first of all as an American. If the Englishmen living in fifteen colonies scattered from Newfoundland and Nova Scotia to Georgia gave themselves any local name, it was not *American;* it was *Virginian* or *Pennsylvanian* or *Carolinian.* The four colonies grouped around Boston did regard themselves as more or less a unit and the people called themselves *New Englanders;* but elsewhere each man thought of himself as a citizen of his own colony.

There were many reasons for this. Each colony had started out on its own and had nothing to do with the others except to take care that none of them gained an advantage. Virginia and Maryland, for example, lay side by side, but one was a royal colony belonging directly to the king, while the other was a palatinate belonging to the Baron of Baltimore who was, of course, a subject of the king. There was a long squabble over which of the two owned the Potomac River, and there was actually a small war over the ownership of Kent Island in Chesapeake Bay.

Also the colonies differed in many other ways besides their form of government. Massachusetts and Virginia were the two most important colonies and they were entirely different. In Massachusetts the soil was thin and stony. In Virginia it was rich and deep. So naturally the Massachusetts men became sailors and fishermen, while the Virginians became farmers. Sailors and fishermen usually live in seaport towns, so Boston became an important place. Farmers usually live scattered through the country, so Virginia developed no important town in the early days.

Difficulty of communication was a third reason why each colony was more or less a unit in itself. Americans in our time can hardly imagine how hard it was to travel on land in those days. Of course there were no paved roads. In most places there were no roads at all, only rough paths through the woods. When the English General Braddock tried to capture Fort Duquesne (now Pittsburgh, Pennsylvania) he had to send an army of men with axes ahead of him, to cut down the trees and make a road over which he could haul his wagons and cannon. This was the first road to what is now a great American city.

Even where there was a road, it was full of ruts and stones and mudholes. Carriages had no steel springs. To ease the bumping a little, the bodies were hung on leather straps attached to the axles. This helped some, but not much. At best, the traveler was jounced and jarred at a rate that quickly tired him out. Of course it was slow; fifteen miles a day was pretty good going, and twenty miles was fast. So to travel five hundred and fifty miles from Boston to Williamsburg, in Virginia, might well take a month. You just didn't go unless you absolutely had to.

On the other hand, at either place you could get on board a ship and, if the wind was right, in three weeks you could be in England with no jouncing and jarring at all, except what you might get from a storm at sea. From either Massachusetts or Virginia a trip to England was quicker and very much easier than a trip from Massachusetts to Virginia. The result was that the people of Boston and the people of Williamsburg both knew more about London than either knew about the other American town.

It was the British Parliament that made the thirteen colonies realize that they really were one country. The Seven Years' War had cost Great Britain a great deal of money, part of which had been spent defending the American colonies against the French and Indians. Parliament felt that the colonies, which were very prosperous by this time, ought to pay at least part of the cost of their own defense. That was only fair, and the colonists might have been willing to pay except for the way Parliament handled the matter.

At this time all the counties and some of the towns in Great Britain had the right to send representatives to Parliament, so all the counties and some of the towns had a say about what laws were made. But the colonies were not allowed to send representatives, so they had no say. Parliament simply enacted whatever laws it saw fit, and the colonists had to obey. This was not so bad as long as the laws applied to all Englishmen alike, whether they lived in England or in Virginia; but when Parliament passed tax laws that applied only to the colonists, not to the people in England, trouble started.

The most famous of these laws, called the Stamp Act, was passed in 1765. In itself, it wasn't a bad law. Today the United States has several stamp acts that people obey without a murmur. For instance, every pack of cigarettes, every deck of playing cards, and every bottle of whiskey, gin, or brandy carries a revenue stamp that the dealer must buy and stick on before it is sold. He adds the cost of the stamp to the price of the article, so in the end it is really the purchaser who pays the tax. The Stamp Act of 1765 required stamps to be stuck on legal documents, insurance policies, ship's papers, licenses, and newspapers and pamphlets, and agents were to be appointed throughout the colonies to sell the stamps.

It was really a convenient way of raising money and the price of the stamps was not too high. That wasn't what caused the trouble. The trouble was that here was a tax law applying to the colonists and not to Englishmen in England, yet the colonists had had no voice in passing it. So they raised the cry, "Taxation without representation is tyranny!" and refused to obey.

The truth is, the colonists were getting pretty tired of being ruled from London. As long as the Indians were really dangerous, especially with the French behind them, there wasn't much the colonists could do about it, because they needed British soldiers; but now that the French and Indian power had been smashed — and the colonists had done a good deal of the smashing themselves — they were not disposed to put up with the bad government Parliament was giving them.

It was too far away. With luck you could reach England in three weeks, but only if the weather was good and the wind blowing in the right direction. It sometimes happened that you got aboard a ship and then lay in the harbor for three weeks before you got a start, because the wind was blowing the wrong way; and it often happened that when you did get to sea you were becalmed or met head winds, and so spent six weeks or more crossing the Atlantic.

Then when you got to London the government might or might not give prompt attention to your business. Parliament and the king's ministers had a great deal to attend to besides the American colonies, which were small and unimportant. So an American might be kept hanging around for months, or even years, before anybody would take time to listen to what he had to say. Then, as likely as not, the man who did listen would not have the least idea what the colonist was talking about.

This was really the root from which all the quarrels grew. Things in America were so different that not one Englishman in a thousand understood what was worrying the colonists. Even when they were quite friendly they often did the wrong thing, simply because they didn't understand; and when they were not friendly they brushed the colonists aside, and there was nothing the colonists could do about it.

Of course when an American, who felt that what he asked was right and reasonable, couldn't get any satisfaction in London, he was likely to decide that the English hated the colonists. On the other hand, when an Englishman, who felt that such laws as the Stamp Act were right and reasonable, found that the colonists would not obey, he was likely to decide that the colonists were born lawbreakers who needed to be taught a lesson. This misunderstanding grew worse and worse until, ten years after the Stamp Act, a very great Englishman, Dr. Samuel Johnson, could say of Americans: "They are a race of convicts, and ought to be thankful for anything we allow them short of hanging."

To top it all, in 1760 a young fool became the king of England. Because he sat on the throne once occupied by Elizabeth the Great he thought he ought to have the same cheerful obedience that the people had given Elizabeth. This King George (the third one of that name) could never see that the difference between him and the great queen was that she knew how to rule a kingdom and he didn't. From the very start almost everything he did was wrong. He was not wicked, he was just stupid; but the people in America didn't know that, and the longer he reigned the surer they became that he was a monster of wickedness. The people in England did not feel that way, but even they knew that he was a pretty bad king. In the end he lost his mind altogether — not that he ever had much to lose — and they had to lock him up and name a regent to run the kingdom.

There was one mistake which both sides made, and neither could realize that it was a mistake. It was thinking that a man born and growing to manhood in America was an Englishman simply because he spoke English and called himself a subject of the king. He was not an Englishman, he was an American; but for a long time most of the people would not admit it. The Stamp Act forced them to admit it. Here was a law that was as unjust to Virginia as it was to Massachusetts, which made Virginia and Massachusetts realize for the first time that they were in the same boat.

The Stamp Act didn't last long. Thirteen colonies flatly refused to obey it. When the stamps came over from England nobody would buy them. The men who had been appointed agents to sell them, who were usually prominent men because it was an important job, found themselves in serious trouble. Mobs attacked their houses. Some were almost killed and several were run out of the country. Practically all resigned in a great hurry.

In England members of Parliament were astonished at the outburst, but they were not unreasonable. If the Americans felt that way about it, they would repeal the law, and they did. But they went on to other laws that were as bad or worse, because they were based on the same mistake — the mistake of thinking that the Americans were Englishmen living abroad, who needed what Englishmen needed, wanted what Englishmen wanted, and would act as Englishmen acted.

That simply wasn't true. It was not that the Americans wished to be different. Most of them not only thought of themselves as Englishmen but did not care to be anything else. But they *were* something else. America was not England and many laws that worked well enough in England wouldn't work at all in this country; so the demand that the colonies make their own laws was reasonable, although it looked like rebellion against the king.

One great mistake that Parliament and the king made was not made by the wisest Englishmen: believing that the colonists ought to be content to work for England first and for themselves afterward. The colonists, of course, wished to work for themselves first and for England afterward. Anybody would. Wise men knew that anybody would, and said so to the king and Parliament. Nevertheless, Parliament made laws requiring that nearly everything the colonists sold must be sold in England, and everything they bought must be bought in England — knives, for instance, and some kinds of cloth, and many other things. It was all right for the colonists to dig and smelt the ore, and to raise the wool; but it was unlawful for them to forge the iron into knives and weave the wool into cloth. That had to be done in England, so that Englishmen would get the profit.

Some Englishmen saw that this was all wrong. At the time there were living in England three great statesmen, William Pitt, Edmund Burke, and Charles James Fox. All of them tried to tell the king and Parliament what a mistake they were making, but it was of no use. Parliament was stubborn and King George III was even more stubborn. So they went right ahead, piling one bad law on another for ten years after the end of the Seven Years' War.

The result was that in America more and more people began to think that the British government hated the colonists, and they began to hate the British government. The more angry they became with the British, the more clearly they saw that they must all stand together. The set of laws regulating trade bore down most heavily on the colonies engaged in trade. The chief of these was Massachusetts, where there was not much farming, but a great deal of shipping and fishing. When English law forbade the

ships of Boston to go where they wished and sell their fish where they could get the best price, Boston found it hard to live at all and the Bostonians' tempers got very hot indeed.

Still not understanding what the trouble was about, the British government did the wrong thing. Instead of carefully examining the whole matter and giving the colonists the right to manage their own affairs, the government sent two regiments of infantry and some artillery to Boston to frighten the people into obeying. But it didn't work. Instead of being frightened, they were made more furious than ever. Whenever soldiers off duty went into the town, they had fights with civilians and sometimes these fights became riots. In 1770 some toughs picked on a soldier who was standing sentry at a public building; when the man couldn't endure it any longer, he called out the guard, and the arrival of the guard brought a street crowd. Just what happened after that has always been disputed, because there was a lot of yelling and cursing and jostling. Somebody began throwing stones and somebody — no one ever knew who — gave the soldiers the order to fire, which they did. Three of the crowd were killed on the spot, and two others later died of their wounds.

This is what is known as the Boston Massacre, although it was actually a street riot. That is the sort of thing that was going on at one end of the country. Near the other end, in North Carolina, there was an actual war between the governor and the back-country farmers, ending in 1771 in a battle between government troops and two thousand farmers calling themselves Regulators. The farmers were scattered, and the governor hanged one Regulator on the field and six others after a trial for treason. This was more like a real massacre, although the anger of the Regulators was aimed more at the local government than at the king and Parliament. It does show, though, how hatred of the government was spreading from one end of America to the other.

The most important effect of such things as the Boston Massacre and the Regulators' War was not that they made everybody furious. The important thing was the way it showed the colonies that they had to get together. Massachusetts and North Carolina were hundreds of miles apart. They had different climates, they had different soils, their people lived different kinds of lives. But in one thing they were alike — they were both being roughly handled by the British, and that likeness was more important than their differences.

Smart men in all the colonies began to see this and one, in particular, did something about it. In Boston Samuel Adams (he had a cousin named John, who was a greater man and became second President of the United States, but John Adams hadn't done much yet) persuaded the people to set up a committee of twenty-one men whose duty it would be to make a record of everything the British did to Boston and send this record up and down the country. The idea seemed a good one and soon every colony had one of these Committees of Correspondence. Of course there was no telegraph then, and newspapers were few and small, so it was hard for one colony to find out what was going on in another.

The Committees fixed that. When a crowd of men painted to look like Mohawk Indians raided a ship that had come into port after Parliament had laid a special tax on tea, and threw into Boston harbor all the tea on board — 342 chests of it — the news was soon known all up and down the country. It was also imitated. In New York they also threw tea into the harbor, and at Annapolis, Maryland, they not only threw the tea overboard, they burned the ship.

So the thing happened that usually happens when wise men lose control of the government and the stupid take over. When one side got tough, the other got tougher, and soon it was plain that in the end they would probably have to fight it out. No one colony could possibly stand up against the British Army and Navy, but there was a bare chance that

thirteen might. The problem was to get them together, so that the British would have to fight them
all at once and not destroy them one at a time.

That was not easy. It was, in fact, so very hard to
do that they never did succeed in accomplishing it
completely. The colonial population in those days
was a long way from being entirely composed of
wise and good men. In every thousand people there
were probably as many cheats and liars and other
kinds of rogues as there are in every thousand Americans today.

Their quarrel with Great Britain was not the only
one. The colonies also had quarrels among themselves. The squabble between Maryland and Vir-

ginia over the Potomac has already been mentioned, but there were many others. New York and New Jersey, for instance, were in constant rows over the harbor lying between them. New Jersey and Pennsylvania had more than one fuss over the Delaware River. Nor was it always a matter of boundary lines. One colony was always trying to squeeze another over some matter of trade. Virginia, for instance, holding the two capes at the mouth of the Chesapeake Bay, charged a toll on every Maryland ship that passed between them, and North Carolina, with no good harbors, had to make a payment on all goods she shipped through Virginia ports. The small colonies, Rhode Island and Delaware, were always suspecting that the big ones, Pennsylvania and Virginia, were trying to put something over on them; and all too often they were themselves trying to put something over on the big ones.

Perhaps they never would have been able to stand together if a foolish act of Great Britain had not made them see that it was either stand together or fall one by one. On June 1, 1774, the British closed the port of Boston and announced that it would remain closed until the tea that had been thrown into the harbor was paid for. Closing the port meant starving the town into submission; and if it could happen to Boston it could happen to any other town.

This started a movement for a great meeting of all the colonies to see what could be done about it. So in September, 1774, twelve colonies — all except Georgia — sent 56 delegates to the halfway point between Massachusetts and Georgia, which was considered to be Philadelphia, where they met in a hall belonging to the association of carpenters. This was the First Continental Congress. It sat for a month and adopted resolutions declaring that all the laws that tried to make the colonists subject to the will of Parliament were not really laws at all and ought not to be obeyed. They encouraged the people of Boston and advised all the colonies to raise troops to defend themselves.

But there the First Continental Congress stopped. At that time nobody except a few wild fellows wanted war, and a great many colonists still held to the old idea that God had appointed the king, therefore rebellion against the king was rebellion against God. Two or three hundred years earlier everybody had believed in this divine right of kings; but as time passed and people learned more and more about kings, they quit believing in divine right. When they found themselves with a thoroughly bad king or even a half-crazy one, such as George III, the idea that God had appointed him didn't seem true, and most people gave it up.

Still, when people have believed anything for a long time, they find it hard to rid their minds of it even when their common sense tells them that it can't be true. Most of the colonists no longer believed that divine right was anything but nonsense, yet there was something about fighting against the king that they didn't like at all, even when he was a bad king. That is why the First Continental Congress stopped where it did; but before it adjourned in October, 1774, it agreed to meet again in May.

As the winter passed things went from bad to worse, and in all the colonies they began to organize and drill military companies. In New England, especially, a great many men who were not soldiers at all took time to learn to drill. Each man got a gun and kept it by him; and each agreed to be ready at all times to pick up his gun and join the company on one minute's notice. They called them minutemen. They were not trained fighters, but they were brave, they knew how to shoot, and there were a lot of them.

So the commander of the British troops in Boston became nervous. He had plenty of soldiers to hold the town, but the country round about was swarming with minutemen, and other companies of militia were coming from nearby colonies, which made it seem likely that real trouble might be on the way.

Then he got word that the colonists were assembling a great quantity of gunpowder and weapons at Concord, a village twenty-one miles from Boston. Thereupon the British general, named Gage, decided to break up the business then and there; so one night he called out 700 men and sent them to Concord to seize the stores.

Gage tried to move secretly, but the colonists were watching and sent three horsemen, Paul Revere, William Dawes, and Dr. Samuel Prescott, to give warning. Revere was captured five miles short of Concord, Dawes ran into a patrol and had to turn back, but Dr. Prescott got through, so the Americans hastily loaded their stuff into wagons and got it out of Concord. Years later the poet Longfellow, not knowing the circumstances, wrote a poem giving all the credit to Paul Revere, leaving Dawes and Prescott out; so to this day most people think of it as Paul Revere's Ride, although it should be Prescott's, if any one man's.

In the meantime the British advance guard had reached Lexington, sixteen miles from Boston, without any trouble, but there it found seventy armed minutemen assembled on the village green. The British commander, Major Pitcairn, ordered them to drop their arms and disperse. They began to disperse but they didn't drop the guns, and while they were filing off, somebody — we never have known who — fired a shot. This was too much for the British soldiers and, without orders from Pitcairn, they let go a volley. Eight Americans were killed and, although a few fired back, only one British soldier was wounded.

Then the main body of the British, under Lieutenant Colonel Smith, came up and they pushed on to Concord. By that time only a small and scattered supply of gunpowder and weapons was left there, but the war was on. That day, April 19, 1775, was the beginning of the end of the British king's rule. Word of the skirmish at Lexington had spread fast,

and 4000 minutemen came swarming to both sides of the road that the British had to take to get back to Boston. They did not fight in any regular order. They lay behind trees, stone fences, houses — anything that would afford cover — and each man fired as he saw fit. If Gage had not sent reinforcements from Boston, Smith would have been finished; as it was, 73 of his men were killed, 26 were missing, and 174 wounded — a total of 273 out of 700, a terrible casualty rate.

So there it was — from that day on we were at war, and nobody can say exactly who began it. Lieutenant Porter, who commanded the minutemen at Lex-

ington, did not attack the British; on the other hand, Major Pitcairn did not give the order to fire on the Americans. Apparently the soldiers on both sides started the fight among themselves without orders from anybody. But if it hadn't happened at Lexington that day, it would almost certainly have happened somewhere else very soon. The two countries simply couldn't understand each other. That always means trouble and often means war, and it really makes little difference where the first shot is fired or who fires it. The misunderstanding, not the shot, is the cause.

After the fight on April 19 — called the Battle of Lexington, although Lexington was about the only place from Concord to Boston where they did not fight — militia companies from the rest of Massachusetts and from the adjoining colonies hurried to the aid of the minutemen until, by the time the Second Continental Congress met on May 10, there were nearly 10,000 armed men around Boston keeping the British penned in the town. That meant that war was already raging, but still nobody wanted to admit it.

It was plain that things had to be straightened out somehow. The men around Boston were organized, some into independent companies, some into battalions, some into regiments, each obeying its own officers and paying no attention to any others. Half of them never knew what the other half were doing and they were continually getting in each other's way. You can't run an army like that, so the first thing Congress did was to decide that these people should no longer be divided into Massachusetts minutemen and Connecticut militia and New Hampshire volunteers and so on, but that they should all be the Army, not of any one colony, but of the whole continent, and should be commanded by one general appointed by Congress. Since all the colonies were to join in supplying the army with food, uniforms, guns, and ammunition, they called it the Continental Army.

Then John Adams, cousin of the Samuel Adams already mentioned, had a very bright idea. Virginia was by far the largest and richest of the colonies and Pennsylvania was next, but the fighting so far had all been in Massachusetts, a long way from Virginia and Pennsylvania, and Massachusetts badly needed help from both. So Adams, himself a Massachusetts man, started a movement to get a man from Virginia named Commander-in-Chief of the Continental Army, mainly to keep Virginia interested in the war.

Fortunately Virginia had a good man, in fact the best possible man for the job. He was a planter, not an army officer, but during the various Indian wars he had seen a lot of hard service and learned a great deal about soldiering in America, which was very different from making war anywhere else in the world. His name was George Washington, and he was already in Philadelphia as a delegate to Congress from Virginia. As soon as Congress voted to make him commander of the Continental Army he started for Boston; and except for very short visits he didn't get back to his Virginia home for nearly eight years.

Before he reached the Army — while Congress was still voting on his commission — there had been another big fight. Gage now had three other British

major generals to help him; they were Sir William Howe, Sir Henry Clinton, and General John Burgoyne. Toward the middle of June the Americans began to build earthworks on two hills across the Charles River from Boston, Breed's Hill, nearest Boston, and Bunker Hill, behind Breed's. Gage decided that he had better break that up before the Americans mounted cannon on the two hills and began to fire into the town. So on June 17 he sent Howe across the river with 2400 men. Howe did the job; he captured both hills, but at terrific cost. Before he took Breed's Hill he was thrown back twice, and Clinton had to come over with more men to help him. At that, the main reason they succeeded was that the Americans ran out of gunpowder.

With our strange habit of giving battles the wrong name we call this the Battle of Bunker Hill, although four fifths of the fighting was on Breed's. It was very important, not because the Americans won, for they didn't, but because they learned a great deal about how to fight the British. Any army that goes into battle and loses ten per cent of its men has been in a hot fight, and on this day Howe lost nearly forty per cent (1024 out of 2400) while the Americans lost only 397. Gage realized that with a few more victories like that he wouldn't have any army left; while the Americans discovered that by using their rifles from behind earthworks they could stop the finest British infantry.

So when, on July 3, 1775, George Washington took formal command of the Army in the neighborhood of Boston, the war had actually been raging for three months. It would be exactly a year and one day before Congress made up its mind to accept the fact.

CHAPTER EIGHT

America Is Born

THEY FOUGHT for seven years, but the fighting was not what made us Americans, although people often say it did. We were Americans before the war began, but we didn't know it. The war made us know it, at least in part. Many years were to pass before we were sure of it, and to this day some people doubt that we really are one nation.

But by the time the British formally gave up — that was in 1783 — we did know that we were not simply Englishmen living away from home. That was the way the colonists had looked upon themselves, just as today an engineer who goes to build an oil refinery in Venezuela doesn't doubt that he is an American, even though he may stay out of the country for years at a time.

If you had asked George Washington, when he took command of the Army around Boston in 1775, to describe himself, he would have said that he was an English gentleman from Virginia; but if you had asked him the same question in 1783, he would have said that he was an American gentleman from Virginia. The truth is, he had been an American from the day he was born, but it was the war that made him realize it.

The war also proved that one state, standing alone, is helpless, but that when all stick together they are hard to beat. As soon as the British found that they had a real war on their hands they got out of Boston, because that was no place from which to fight all thirteen colonies. It was too far north. So they assembled two armies and a naval fleet at Halifax, in Nova Scotia, and planned a pincer movement. They would send one army up the St. Lawrence River to where the Richelieu River comes in. From that point it would push south along Lake Champlain and Lake George to the Hudson, and down the Hudson to Albany.

In the meantime, the fleet would take the other army to New York, and from there it would push up the Hudson to meet the army from Canada at Albany. That would cut the country in two, and each end could then be beaten separately.

It was a good plan on paper, but it didn't work. The men in London who did the planning didn't know enough about the country between the St. Lawrence and the Hudson. To march 7000 men 250 miles is no easy job, even when you go through open country with good roads. When you have no roads and must go through thick forest it is many times harder; yet that is what the British commander, General Burgoyne, had to do.

The commander of the other army, General Howe, had a much easier job and did it very well. The fleet brought his army to New York and landed it on Long Island. There Washington made the mistake of trying to stop him. Washington had as many men as Howe and there is no doubt that, man for man, they were as strong and as brave as the British. But they were not trained soldiers, except for a few, and when the battle began they got excited.

Howe sent part of his army around the left end of the American line. What the Americans should have done was to extend their line or, if they couldn't do that, let it bend back slowly, always holding together and facing the British. But both officers and men got confused. Some units fell back, but some refused to budge. That opened holes in the line and the British poured through. The units that stood fast were surrounded and quickly killed or captured, and the next thing Washington knew, the enemy were getting behind his main army and he was almost trapped. He had to order a fast retreat and managed to get most of his army across the East River into Manhattan Island.

But it was a near thing. It taught Washington that until his army was much better trained he could not risk a stand-up fight with the British veterans. His only hope was to wear them down. So he retreated slowly up the Hudson, fighting small battles at Harlem Heights and White Plains, but not really trying to hold anywhere.

Then Howe didn't know what to do. He could drive the Americans up the Hudson, but what was the use? He couldn't hope to drive them all the way to Canada, and Burgoyne hadn't even started yet. In fact, he did not get started until the next summer. So Howe turned south and pushed Washington all across New Jersey. Washington did what he could, but the British army rolled on in spite of him. However, all it did was to capture a lot of ground, and when Howe sent the bulk of his troops back to winter quarters in New York, Washington fell on isolated detachments at Trenton and Princeton and wrecked them. Still, that wasn't winning the war. Howe was in New York, Burgoyne was in Canada, and the pincer plan was still possible.

It went to pieces when Burgoyne finally hacked his way down through the wilderness and reached the Hudson but got there almost exhausted. His supplies were cut off, his ammunition was running out, and his men were too tired by the long march to be able to fight effectively. Thousands of American militia were swarming around him, and at Saratoga he surrendered to the American commander, General Gates, whom Washington had sent to oppose him.

All this time the nations of Europe had been watching the struggle with great interest, and none more closely than the king of France, who had never forgiven England for the beating he had taken in the Seven Years' War, which ended in 1765. All Europeans who loved liberty sympathized with the colonists, and some enthusiastic young officers came over to help. They were of various nations. There were Baron von Steuben and Baron de Kalb, both Germans, although De Kalb had served in the French army. There was Count Pulaski, a Pole. But especially there was a swarm of young Frenchmen, led by the Marquis de Lafayette, a nobleman with many friends at the court of King Louis. Lafayette not only helped with the fighting, he talked with important people close to the king urging France to join in the war.

The king of France did not want to join a movement that would soon be squelched by the British

army. He didn't mind creating trouble for the king
of England by helping the Americans with money
and guns and gunpowder and whatever else they
needed, but war was a more serious matter. So he
acted as Elizabeth the Great had acted when Drake
and the others were raiding the Spanish colonies —
he pretended not to know about it. A trading company, supposed to be Spanish, was organized and
shipped military supplies to the Americans. When
England protested, the French king coolly pointed
out that he couldn't help what a lot of Spanish merchants were doing, and nobody could prove that the
company was getting its money from the king.

But when news came that one British army had
surrendered and the other hadn't done much, the
French decided that the Americans really could
fight, and therefore were worth supporting. So they
sent over a good army under an able general, the
Count de Rochambeau, and from that time on the
war went steadily against the British.

Howe could still hit. Before the arrival of the
French, he sent an army from New York up Chesapeake Bay, landed near Elkton, Maryland, and
smashed into Philadelphia. Washington tried to stop
him at Brandywine Creek and again at German-
town, and was badly mauled at both places. But although Philadelphia was the capital of the country

and he had captured it, Howe found that it did him
little good. Disgusted, he quit, and Sir Henry Clinton took his place.

Clinton decided to try from the south, so he sent
his best man, Lord Cornwallis, with a strong army to
Charleston. Cornwallis smashed through South Carolina, met Gates, the victor at Saratoga, at Camden,
whipped him soundly, and moved up toward North
Carolina. So Washington sent *his* best man, Nathan-
ael Greene, to the south. Greene couldn't whip Cornwallis, but he could sting him badly, and he did, in
battle after battle up through the Carolinas almost
to the Virginia line. Then at Guilford Courthouse
there was so furious a fight that Cornwallis lost more
than a quarter of his troops; so although Greene had
retreated from the field, the British general gave up
the idea of pushing farther north and marched down
to the sea to get reinforcements from Clinton.
Greene let him go and went to work cleaning up the
Carolinas.

Lafayette and Von Steuben were commanding in
eastern Virginia when Cornwallis got there, and
Washington sent General Anthony Wayne to help.
Gradually they wore Cornwallis down and eventu-
ally penned him up on the peninsula between two
rivers, with Yorktown at the end.

All this time Washington and Rochambeau had

been watching Clinton in New York; but when they heard that Cornwallis was holed up at Yorktown, they made a rapid march south, so beautifully conducted that they were almost at the head of Chesapeake Bay before Clinton knew they had moved. He rushed help to Cornwallis by sea but it never got there, because the French Admiral De Grasse had come up from the West Indies and he drove the British back off the Virginia capes at the entrance of Chesapeake Bay. Then De Grasse sailed into the bay and past Yorktown, brought Washington and Rochambeau down in ships, and they had Cornwallis.

For three weeks he put up a good fight, but he really never had a chance, and on October 19, 1781, he surrendered. That ended the war, although it was two years before the peace treaty was finally signed.

America had learned by then that it was a separate and independent nation. Its people also knew then that no one of the thirteen states could hope to stand alone against a first-rate European army. Virginia, Pennsylvania, and Massachusetts, in that order, were the strongest, yet when the British army struck each of them in turn it went down like a house of cards. It took the united effort of all thirteen finally to wear down the British strength.

Those things the War of Independence, which we call the Revolution, did teach us, but it didn't make

us Americans. That had been done before. It didn't create the nation as we know it now, for that was done afterward.

There was another thing that the war did for the American people that was nearly as important as getting rid of the British king. The war taught the people to know George Washington and taught Washington to know the people.

In 1775 only the Virginians knew much about the man. The people in Massachusetts and those in Georgia had heard of him as a good Indian fighter, and perhaps some of them knew that he was a rich landowner who had managed his estate remarkably well. On his part, he knew the Virginians and the country as far up as Pittsburgh, but not much more. But after seven years of war, there was no man known to so many people in every one of the thirteen states, and no man who knew the people of all the states so thoroughly.

When victory was won at last, the army was strongly in favor of making him king of America, and it probably could have been done, for at the time only those who had studied the histories of Greece and Rome knew much about republics, and what they knew was not altogether favorable. We had always lived under a king, so it seemed the natural way for a country to be governed. Washington would have made a good one, so if he had said the word it is quite likely that he would have been given a crown. But the word he said was no, and he said it so flatly and firmly that the movement collapsed at once. There was no pretense about it, either. He did not in the least want to be king. He wanted to go home and run his farm, and that was all in the world he did want.

Most historians agree that George Washington was the greatest American that ever lived, but when you try to pin down exactly what it was that made him great, it is surprisingly hard to do. He was not the greatest general. Napoleon, Julius Caesar, Alexander the Great were far better, and it was Robert E. Lee, not Washington, that a British critic called "the greatest captain of the English-speaking race." He was not a great lawgiver, such as Moses and Lycurgus and Solon; he didn't write the Declaration of Independence or the Constitution. He could not do as many things as Jefferson, he could not argue as well as Hamilton or speak as eloquently as Patrick Henry. He was not as witty as Franklin or as learned as John Adams. Yet we all admit that he was greater than any of them.

He was a good man, but a long way from being a saint. In the army, when someone did something terribly stupid or cowardly, Washington could and did swear in a way that made the soldiers gasp. He could be hard, too. Mutineers and deserters he had shot without mercy, and when the British Major André was caught carrying messages for the traitor, Arnold, Washington wouldn't even let him be shot — the death of a soldier — but had him hanged — the death of a spy. In time of peace he loved to attend the races and balls at Annapolis. He liked dancing and a good dinner and good wine. He went to church regularly, yet never was regarded as extremely pious.

Thus far, we have a man with all the good qualities, but none in the very highest degree; and a man with some faults, but none extreme enough to be

called a vice. All this adds up to make an able man, but that is about all. Yet we call him the greatest American, so it is plain that there must be something else that has not been mentioned.

There are two qualities thus far left out. In themselves they would make a good man, but perhaps not a very great one. Added to everything else that Washington had, they lift him a notch or two higher than any other man who has lived in this country. One is the fact that when Washington saw that something was his duty he did it to the utmost limit of his ability, and at no matter what cost. The other is the fact that he never expected or desired any reward for doing his duty.

That is to say, he never desired any reward from other men. He expected and he desired a reward, and he got it, but it was nothing that any other man could see or hear or touch or taste or smell. It was nothing except the pleasure in his own mind that doing his duty gave him. When you find a man of whom it is really true that the pleasantest thing in the world to him is knowing that he has done his duty, then you have found a very great man. Because this was added to all the rest, Washington stands above every other American.

We have spoken of the war with England as the

Revolution. Some people object to calling it by that
name. They say that a real revolution upsets everything, not merely the form of government but everything else, including manners and customs, property
rights, social classes, and so on. In our country everything went on as before except that we changed the
government from a monarchy to a republic. Therefore, they say, the war should be called the War for
Independence, not the Revolution. I think they are
wrong. We changed a great deal more than the government, and it was a real revolution.

After the war Americans knew that they had become a different nation from the British. But the war
did not tell them what to do about it. That they
had to figure out for themselves, and it took them a
long time, a great deal of argument, and the making
of many mistakes before they got a clear idea of
how to act.

In fact, the argument still goes on, but in these
days it is mostly about small matters. As for the
really big things, we now know pretty well what is
the American way of acting and what is not. The
way in which we came to agree on the big things
is the way in which we came to be Americans. It
was not done by fighting but by thinking things out;
and it was not done all at once but over a long period
of time. It is not yet finished. It will never be fin-

ished. As long as a man lives he changes a little every day, and the same thing is true of a nation.

We have only to look around to see that all babies are pretty much alike, but when they change from babies to children they become different. A boy grows bigger and stronger until he reaches what we call his full growth, after which, although he continues to change, we don't notice it much. He remains the same person, even though his once black hair may turn white and his once smooth face may become wrinkled. A nation lives far longer than any man, but it goes through very much the same stages. The United States right now is not exactly what it was in George Washington's day or in Abraham Lincoln's day or even in Franklin D. Roosevelt's day, but it is the same nation. It was born on July 4, 1776, but it was thirteen years old before it began to look the way it looks now.

Seven of these were war years, but the other six were a time of confusion and quarreling and general mess that in some ways was worse than a time of war. As long as the fighting lasted, everybody was intent on that and thought little about anything else. It was plain from the beginning that the British could easily defeat any one of the thirteen colonies separately, so they agreed that the Continental Congress should be the general government of all thirteen.

They drew up a formal contract called the Articles of Confederation, setting forth the duties of Congress and the duties of each state. But Congress argued for a year over what should go into the Articles, and it took three years more to get all the states to ratify it. Maryland held out until the bigger states gave up their claims to land beyond the Appalachian Mountains. Maryland had no such lands, but Connecticut and Pennsylvania claimed some, North Carolina extended, in theory, to the Mississippi River, and Virginia claimed everything from the North Carolina line to the Great Lakes.

There were still very few white people in the whole region, but envious Maryland feared that in time to come she would be overwhelmed by such gigantic states, and demanded that all unsettled lands beyond the mountains should be the general property of the Confederation. So Virginia ceded her claims to Congress in January, 1781, and Maryland ratified the Articles. North Carolina gave up what is now Tennessee in 1784, and gladly, too, because the settlers there had revolted and set up their own "State of Franklin," and it cost North Carolina a pretty penny to subdue them.

But as soon as the fighting was over and people began to think about other things than victory it became plain that the Articles of Confederation simply would not work as a real government. While there was a British army threatening everybody, the states had to forget their private squabbles and stand together behind Washington; but as soon as the Redcoats — our name for the British soldiers — disappeared, it became apparent that the thirteen states were a long way from perfect. Every kind of ugly and wicked desire appeared. Jealousy and greed and hatred showed up in many places. It soon became clear that some states would, if they could, tyrannize over others as brutally as the king ever did.

New York and New Jersey quarreled over who should own New York Bay, which lies between them. The New England states laid taxes, called duties, on everything brought in from other states. Maryland, by the old charter, owned the Potomac River to the south bank and refused to allow the Virginians to fish in the river; but Virginia owned the capes at the mouth of the Chesapeake Bay and refused to let ships come up to Annapolis and Baltimore without paying duties to Virginia. Each of the states could issue its own paper money, but there was nothing to make the people in the next state take it and frequently they would not. When they did they usually took it at a sharp discount, so if a man crossed a state line the money in his pocket lost part of its value.

Worst of all, each state was supposed to pay a different amount to support the expenses of Congress and repay the money borrowed by Congress during the war. Some of them paid only part of what they were supposed to contribute and some paid nothing at all; and there was no power to force them to do so. The result was that Congress was getting deeper and deeper into debt, and nobody wanted to accept its paper money. The soldiers of Washington's Army had been paid in paper money issued by the Continental Congress and therefore called continentals, and as time passed these bills lost value steadily, which meant that the soldiers were cheated out of their pay. It got so bad that a new slang term was invented. When something had no value at all, people said it was "not worth a continental," and sometimes you hear that phrase even now.

To make things worse, some rascals began to issue counterfeit continentals. When a bank teller discovered one of these bad bills, it was his duty to take a rubber stamp and stamp across the face of it the Latin word *damnatus*, meaning "condemned." This made the bill utterly worthless, and added a word to the popular phrase, which became, "not worth a continental damn."

Everyone who did any thinking soon saw that this sort of thing could not go on or the country would

fall to pieces. So all sorts of groups began to get together to see if something couldn't be done. One met
at George Washington's home, Mount Vernon, on
the banks of the Potomac, to straighten out the quarrel between Virginia and Maryland. They did. Maryland agreed to allow the Virginians to fish and take
oysters in the river, and Virginia agreed to allow
Maryland ships to pass through the capes without
paying duty.

That being done — it happened in 1785 — they
began to talk about the general situation, and won-
dered why a small group couldn't get together and
straighten out the other problems. It seemed such a
good idea that on their own responsibility they issued a call for delegates from every state to meet at
Annapolis, Maryland, the next year.

It was not a success. Only five states were represented, by twelve delegates. (Curiously enough
Maryland, where the convention met, didn't send a
man). But New York, New Jersey, Pennsylvania,
Delaware, and Virginia did send delegates. One of
them from New York was Alexander Hamilton, who
wrote a very strong report calling on all the states
to send delegates to a new convention at Philadelphia on the second Monday in May, 1787, to consider and recommend what could be done to make
the government work.

This report was sent to all the states and to Congress. Congress gabbled about it from September, 1786, until February, 1787 — almost five months — and then issued a feeble approval, saying that it was "expedient" to consider how the Articles of Confederation could be improved. But, feeble or not, it was approval, and that made the thing official. The delegates who went to Philadelphia were not mere private citizens sitting on Mr. Washington's porch and talking about what they hoped somebody would do. They were representatives backed by the authority of the various states and having the indorsement of Congress. Whatever they did would still have to be approved by the country, but it was no longer mere talk, it was action.

At last the United States of America was beginning to live.

Index

*Indicates illustrations

INDEX